COMPLETE GUIDE TO
STARTING
A USED
BOOKSTORE

Old Books Into Gold

Dale L. Gilbert

This book is dedicated

to Marie, whom I loved

first and best of all.

Library of Congress Cataloging-in-Publication Data

Gilbert, Dale L.
   Complete guide to starting a used book store.

   1. Antiquarian booksellers. 2. Booksellers and
bookselling. 3. New business enterprises. I. Title.
II. Title: Complete guide to starting a used bookstore.
Z286.A55G53 1986   070.5   86-17198
ISBN 0-936894-28-8

Published by
Upstart Publishing Co.
12 Portland St.
Dover, NH 03820
(603) 749-5071

Contents

9
SECRET OF MAINTAINING
A QUALITY OFFERING

10
SALES MADE OUTSIDE THE STORE

11
HIRING HELP THAT WON'T HURT

12
TREATING YOUR SPECIAL BOOKS
IN SPECIAL WAYS

FOREWORD

I love to read any new material I can find on book collecting and book selling. Most are chock full of charming anecdotes about the eccentricities of the trade. I've learned something useful from each of them.

Dale Gilbert's "Complete Guide to Staring a Used Bookstore" is the one book I wish I had read before starting in the book business. It is one of the few "Complete Guides" which lives up to its claim.

Only pure luck has prevented me from going under from the weight of many colossal blunders. Had I heeded Gilbert's practical advice, the road would have been much smoother.

In twelve years in the book trade, I have witnessed the demise of many colleagues. Some were good book-people and poor business people. Others were the opposite. A degree is not required to hang a shingle in our trade, not even a degree in common sense. Gilbert's nuts and bolts approach would greatly assist any novice or veteran wishing to succeed.

Read and heed the sections on buying, site location, pricing, advertising and employees. The advice is priceless and could make the difference between success and failure. After rereading the book, I've decided to slice and pare the stock which gathers the most dust on my shelves. The results have been immediately gratifying.

So for you bibliophiles whose careers are nasty, brutish and short, or if you fantasize about opening a shop from your overflowing shelves, do it. But do it properly. Read this book, follow the author's guidelines and you'll be on the right track. Like Gilbert, I wouldn't trade the out-of-print book trade for any other. Every day is a joyous learning experience, filled with colorful characters. And, there's always room for one more.

Doug Robertson
The Book Guild of Portsmouth
Portsmouth, New Hampshire

Introduction

I felt compelled to write the following book partly out of love and partly out of anger. As you read, I think this will become apparent. Love because the antiquarian book industry has given me most of what I wanted from life, and not just in in the corporal sense. Anger because the business is so simple and straightforward a half-bright twelve-year-old could be successful in it and yet the vast majority of used book dealers somehow manage to bitch the whole thing up.

When I began in this business fifteen years ago I was just coming from a decade with one of the so-called Fortune 500 companies; that's supposed to be the stairway to success in this country, isn't it? Well, the truth is I was depressed, sadly disillusioned and damn near broke after working like a fool for Big Brother for ten long years. I'd been a collector of first editions of my favorite authors for years and more as a source of comfort that security I drifted into the antiquarian book business as a mail-order dealer. Little did I know how generously fate was to deal with me from that point on. I'm not comfortable playing the game some how-to authors do, boasting about how much money they made. On the other hand, if you are to appraise the worth of what I'm offering you within this book, you need some specifics. All I intend to say is that in the first six months after leaving my job with one of the most admired companies in the country and ten years seniority, I earned three times my highest annual salary. The following year — my first full year in the business — I increased that figure another fifty per cent. I used this money to pay cash for my first store and the rest, as they say, is history.

The body of the book is primarily concerned with the mechanics of how I managed all this; here I'd like to talk about the other, perhaps more important needs being a bookseller has filled in my life. For ten years I carried a leather bag full of free samples of prescription drugs around and gave things away to largely disinterested and surprisingly uninformed doctors. It was not an ennobling experience. But I accepted it because I thought that was how it had to be; as far as I could see everybody felt about the same.

The biggest surprise when I became a bookseller wasn't the money; it was the PRIDE and the SATISFACTION I felt as a tangible thing, a rosy glow I still enjoy today. Oh, it's easy to say the money wasn't important but it certainly was then. Part of that rosy glow I'm sure came as the result of knowing I'd never again agonize over paying my bills. Come to think of it, it's amazing how few bills you have to pay when money isn't a problem. That's because you never have to finance anything, I guess.

What I'm trying to tell you is I don't believe there are very many avocations in the world which make you feel as good about yourself and what you do as mine. It's about like having the income of a member of the U.S. House of Representatives but with the satisfactions of a philosopher-teacher. We're not talking about a get-rich-quick scheme in the usual sense, which usually involves some sort of a fast shuffle and the very real possibility of someone getting hurt. If you conduct your business as outlined within the following pages everybody wins. Who deals in a product which does more good and less harm than a bookseller? Who gives better value for the pittance he asks in return? Who belongs to an older, more respected and valuable profession? This is the thing which makes bookselling really special; this is a way of life you can feel good about every moment you're involved with it.

There you have the real wonder of what this book offers. A life-long career which not only warms the belly but the soul as well. I've tried to touch upon the sense of childish wonder and excitement that goes with the territory too. If you decide to take the plunge and open a shop of your own, I hope that child you once were is not too far below the surface. He's going to be one of your main business assets; and he's going to have a ball.

1

Why Get into the Antiquarian Book Business?

Of the many worlds which man did not receive as a gift of nature, but which he created with his own spirit, the world of books is the greatest. . . . Without words, without writing, and without books there would be no history; there could be no concept of humanity.

Hermann Hesse

Imagine you are strolling among the aisles of the largest *NEW* book store in the world. Possibly, it would cover an area of at least fifteen acres. Within its twenty-seven miles of shelving is to be found every single title currently in print in the English language. What a breathtaking and overwhelming sight it would be for those of us who appreciate, even love, books.

Alas, there is not and never will be such a shop. But if there were, that enormous stock would represent a mere 3 per cent of the total number of titles published during the more than five hundred years since the printing of books began. There you have but a single one of the tremendously exciting premises upon which the antiquarian book industry is based. A shop dealing in previously-owned books draws upon the total sum of all books for its rich and varied stock. Think of it! The possibilities are endless and forever intriguing.

Another happy aspect is the fact that more and more avid readers are turning to such shops for their books as the price of new books continues to soar. It is not at all unusual for a reader to wade through five books per week. Even assuming they never purchased a single solitary hardback, that adds up to something around one hundred dollars per month. Is it any wonder they are beginning to seek out shops where the books are not only sold for half price, but they enjoy the privilege of trading them back in again, cutting their cost by yet another half?

Add to that the fact that there are millions of willing buyers hungrily seeking out-of-print books for a host of reasons. Many yearn to complete precious collections of some favorite author. Others are building the most extensive library possible on a subject which fascinates. To some it is the beauty of the books themselves which attracts. Many collect books the way some collect art, using them in the same way, to highlight and dramatize a home or office. Older clients very often retain cherished memories of books they read as children which perhaps influenced their lives. They want very much to have those books again, perhaps to regain some tiny bit of that long-ago childhood.

Then we have those who play the collectable book market as some play the stock market or invest in precious metals. They delight in trying to figure out where the next big jump in values might occur. Investing for profit has its points. A very few years ago some I know guessed right about Stephen King. They now find themselves in the happy position of owning books they paid ten or twelve dollars for which are now worth from three to seven hundred dollars. These are his early titles published by Doubleday. It's certainly more fun to own books while you're waiting for the price to go up than it would be a stock certificate or a silver bar. And the price of admission is low. This market for the antiquarian bookseller is growing; I've actually had clients come to me on orders from their investment advisers to request a list of available books which I considered likely to appreciate substantialy.

There are hundreds of other reasons for the terrific demand for out-of-print books. The result of course is that the entire industry is going to grow geometrically. I can honestly think of no other business that could possibly offer the many rewards of this one, certainly none that is as easy and inexpensive to enter. There are used book stores in just about every city and town in the country. One just opened in the nearby town of Lebanon, Missouri — population 9300. I'm told the shop is doing very well.

But the unfortunate fact is, most of the shops now operating are a disgrace to the industry. They are poorly stocked with shabby, too common, outdated, musty, dirty and totally unsaleable books. They are owned and operated by people who haven't a clue what they're doing. Many are dark and dirty, located in unsuitable places. These are an insult to potential customers; needless to say, they do not flourish. The fact that the market is immense and yet so poorly serviced is the genesis of this book. For those of you who share my great love of books, I want to show you precisely how to convert that noble dream into a highly profitable and exceedingly satisfying career. Imagine yourself in a situation — try to imagine a more ideal one — in which you only have to deal with the readers of the world. To fully appreciate what this means you will have had to be in other kinds of retail sales as I have. In the book business you don't serve the public as a whole as you would in nearly every other type of store. Your clientele is literate, appreciative of the extraordinary service you provide, and in all my years in the business I've yet to receive a bad check. Compare notes on that fact with the owner of your local grocery, liquor, hardware, clothing, furniture or any other type of store you can think of. If you've ever dreamed of turning a delightful avocation into the perfect vocation, this is it!

PROGNOSIS FOR THE FUTURE OF THE INDUSTRY

I read an amazing statistic in an ABA (American Bookseller's Association) article a few years ago. It was stated that there were fewer bookstores in the United States then than there were in colonial times. Sounds incredible, doesn't it? Of course, in colonial times a bookseller was often a man who walked the streets and roads with bags of books strapped around his body. And every printer was also a bookseller. Ben Franklin was a bookseller. Yet isn't it an astounding thought given the small number of people scattered along the Eastern seaboard at the time.

Today there are many times more new book shops in the United States than there are antiquarian shops. The large chains like B. Dalton can almost be counted on to take a prime space in any new shopping center that goes up in any good-sized city if the center is top drawer. Industry newsletters tell us the pendulum is beginning to swing back toward reading. People are reading more than they did a decade ago. No doubt that's part of the reason viewing is off substantially for all three major television networks. Children's reading programs like RIF Reading Is Fundamental are bound to have an effect.

Our high-tech society today is increasingly unforgiving to the functionally illiterate and the poorly read. Nonfiction books of all sorts are pouring off the presses and being gobbled up by an ever more insatiable population of success oriented men and women. With this race for achievement comes the need for more and better fiction. Experts tell us one of the things which preserve our sanity in this pressure-cooker world is the ability to fantasize. Most of us have felt that need, which explains why fiction sales are soaring. Genre fiction from mysteries to fantasy is in great demand. The relatively new, thick historical romances disappear from shelves with amazing speed. And best of all, romance or Harlequin books are being devoured like popcorn. There is no better example of the need to fantasize than to see professional women who are supporters of women's rights fill up a bag with romance books in which the male is dominant and the female always submissive. It's called filling your needs; we all do it. At least we should.

In June, 1984, a group known as B.I.S.G. Book Industry Study Group whose statistics are considered very reliable, published their first report since 1978. It seems, in spite of ever in creasing competition for our leisure time, books are thriving. Fifty-six per cent of the adults in the United States are readers of books. This is an increase of eight million readers since the 1978 report. Better yet, we are reading more now than at the time of the earlier report. The percent age of so-called heavy readers has increased dramatically from 18 per cent to an astounding 35 per cent. Most readers read for pleasure. The study also pointed out 21 per cent of all books read are borrowed, which means reading is actually up even more than increased sales figures indicate.

So the industry as a whole is quite healthy, but what about the previously-owned book shop? Well, that's the best news of all. Unlike the new shop where it has become increasingly difficult for the individual to buck the tide of the big chains, the used shop stands on the threshold of opportunity. The antiquarian book business is so unique and personal it doesn't lend itself to the multiple store approach. You'd appreciate how important this is if you were a new bookstore owner operating in the same town with a chain store who was able to purchase books for less than you because the home office ordered in quantity for all its outlets. That will never happen to a used store owner because he only buys his books from one source — his customers and the general public. Now I'll tell you why the antiquarian book business is just on the brink of a bonanza. *The vast majority of the reading public is just now beginning to become aware the industry exists!* Until very recently there have existed for the most part two distinct types of used book stores. One was the posh antiquarian shop with its shelves of leather and vellum bound tomes priced well beyond the range of the general public. The other was the dingy little Salvation Army-type store where the books were usually just chucked onto the shelf if you were lucky or ranged around the floor in boxes if you weren't. Neither met the needs of most of us and so we coughed up the price of a new book when we really wanted it and swapped among ourselves and maybe went to garage sales in hopes of finding something readable.

Now the stage is set and the timing is right. Wherever you live, if it's large enough to support even one new book store, I can tell you this: there is a hungry market out there waiting to make you or somebody like you very successful. If you will just provide a clean, well-lighted store with books in fine condition you will be very, very pleased with the results. I've watched it happen time and time again; I've done it three times. Don't you think people will be delighted to buy their paperbacks from you for two dollars instead of the four they've been paying? But they won't put up with some dingy hole-in-the-wall to do it.

The really successful antiquarian shops around the country are one of the best kept secrets of the business world. Most of the proprietors are extremely reluctant to give specifics on just how well they're doing and you really can't blame them. If their customers knew, half of them might well run out and start their own.

Let me give you some general statements concerning the future of used book shops: 75 per cent of the shops currently in existence are a disgrace and should not and will not survive if and when proper shops are opened in their area.

The moment a fine used shop with competent management opens in an area it will be supported by more than enough clients to make that shop successful.

The more new shops in a given area the better. This advertises books, encourages reading, and provides books for the used shops. Remember, they can't return them for trade at B. Dalton or Waldenbooks.

The more fine used shops in a given area — believe it or not — the better. This helps promote the cause of used books. Why do you think McDonalds, Burger King and Wendys are always found within a few blocks of one another? Because it's good business, that's why. One of the most powerful marketing concepts I know is to draw as many likely customers as possible into a very limited area. Everyone within that area benefits greatly. Many of the most successful antiquarian shops in the country are within the same block as other similar shops; some in fact are side-by-side. In New York and Los Angeles you can find half a dozen fine stores within a few blocks of each other. These shops are fortunate and invariably are doing well. The reason is simple: buyers know they can see more books by going to those stores than they could going to any one isolated shop.

Used book shops have the above advantage going for them, along with so many others. They really aren't in direct competition with one another. Because of the enormous variety of stock they are able to draw upon, there will be so very little duplication on their shelves. This allows, indeed encourages, close cooperation between them and represents yet another substantial difference between the new and the used shop. New book stores within a given area will tend to have nearly identical stock. This makes them vulnerable to competition and price wars, especially the little independent owner/operator. No previously-owned store owner should ever have to have that sword hanging over his head.

In fact, the used book portion of the industry is growing so much faster than the new books, there are attempts being made to incorporate used books into the new shops. A conference at the 1984 American Booksellers Association Convention in Washington, D.C. was devoted to that very question. Of course it can't be done; certainly not on any meaningful scale. I've seen it tried — it doesn't work. But you can scarcely blame new bookstore operators for wishing. They work with a net profit of something on the order of 2 or 3 per cent. A properly run used store operates very near 50 per cent.

The life expectancy of a *new* best seller is six months to a year but an out-of-print book may never die. In fact, in many cases, interest in the title increases in direct proportion to the number of years it's been unavailable.

To put it simply, the prognosis is excellent! Antiquarian shops are uniquely complete shops, able to serve the public in ways no new shop ever could. They buy your books. They accept them in trade toward different titles. They sell you anything from a half-priced current best seller to a signed first edition. As such attractive stores are beginning to come into existence, more and more people daily are making the happy discovery of the wonders of such shops. There is no doubt in my mind that the coming decade will see the proliferation of previously-owned book stores. The ones that are done intelligently will prosper almost beyond belief. One of the problems of antiquarian booksellers is making the decision of where to stop the growth. It's not an easy judgment. As you will see in the following pages, once the process begins, it becomes self-generating. There are some who have started with minimal shops and let the process carry them on to huge stores doing millions of dollars annually. Others elect not to become involved with large numbers of staff and keep their shops small, electing rather to upgrade stock constantly. Whichever way suits your own needs, if you decide to become a bookseller you will be joining the ranks of a very old and very proud profession. It is a vocation that gives more than most and does less harm than perhaps any other. It doesn't seem to have much attraction for the unscrupulous. It's one of the few remaining businesses where very considerable sums of money change hands strictly on faith. I've accepted checks from people all over the world; I've never felt it necessary to insult anyone by asking to see an ID. By the same token I've sent large sums around the world in payment for books I'd never seen. They always arrived.

It shapes up to be a tremendous growth industry starting right now. Isn't it a fine coincidence it also shapes up to be such a noble, gentle industry. One that doesn't require the hide of an armadillo or the morals of a Dillinger to succeed in. No, this one is for the book people. This is for those of us who could never implement the principles of success being touted these days in books with titles like, *Get Yours By Tramping Over Everybody Else.* Maybe the meek shall inherit the Earth and maybe not, but with the help of this book you can acquire quite a lot of the corporal needs of this life.

SECURITY DURING TROUBLED TIMES

The economic pendulum swings to and fro in this country as it does in all others, though to a lesser degree, thank God. One of the big clouds hanging over the heads of most retailers is the full knowledge that a recession could well spell their doom. There's a an old adage in the world of small business stating the business to be in during hard times is to own a liquor store. For all I know it might be true, for there would appear to be a certain sad logic there. But happily for those of us who cannot picture ourselves in that particular business, there's another somewhat more uplifting enterprise which is also recession proof.

During the recession of the late 1970s I owned an antiquarian book shop in San Diego, California. I saw what was coming and became quite concerned. In discussing it with several other dealers I heard the same thing consistently. Not to worry. It turned out to be true. The tighter things got as the inflation rate skyrocketed, the more new people I saw and the better business became. Customers who never minded paying full retail before began to seek out my store and buy their books for half price. Instead of giving their books away to friends they began to bring them to me for trade credit. People began reading more. I guess in a way it's the same principle as the liquor store mentioned above. When things are rough some people need to drink more; others need to read more. I saw more men buying books on home or auto repairs, hoping to avoid a costly service call. Women sought cook books dealing with inexpensive meals. The sale of self-help books rose as thinking people sought to do something about lifting themselves up to a higher rung on the economic ladder. And the fiction poured out of the shop. What better time to fantasize with a good romance, mystery or whatever suits?

It is true that the sale of books in excess of about one hundred dollars fell off somewhat. Collectors investing before in two or three hundred dollar books began buying one hundred dollar books but the increased activity in general stock more than made up for this slackening. I imagine if one had a shop which stocked only scarce and rare books during that period he would have suffered a drop in sales but we're not concerned within these pages with that sort of operation. I wouldn't suggest anyone contemplate such a store until they've served a suitable apprenticeship. Even then it would have to be located in a rather large metropolitan area to thrive. For the purposes of this book we are concerned with a shop offering largely general stock, though fine collectable material will inevitably come your way and add to your pleasure as well as your profits.

Another major reason the antiquarian book store owner is relatively safe from the vagaries of the economy is because he's in the enviable position of having a business which costs very little to start up. Normally to be earning at the level he is, the used book store owner would have had to invest something over six figures. This book is predicated on the fact that a fine shop can be built, stocked and operated for well under fifteen thousand dollars. Not bad for a business which should easily garner you a true net of three thousand dollars a month within six month of opening the doors. What happens after that is entirely up to you. Right now, unless you've been there you can never appreciate what it means not to have a huge debt service hanging over your head if you had to borrow to start your own business. Even if you had the money in hand you'd still have to consider the loss of all that interest you've suffered by tying up a large amount of money in a business. This, of course, is one of the major reasons why the majority of new businesses fail within the first year. There are precious few businesses — legal ones anyway — where you can be fully operational for so little.

Another big edge is the fact that, not only do you not have any debt service, but in fact you have very few expenses at all. There are no big thirty, sixty, or ninety day billings mushrooming at your wholesalers or your suppliers. You get all your stock from your customers. And most of it costs you nothing because you're going to trade for it. All you've really got to speak of is your rent, utilities, and the small amount you pay in cash for books. Do you begin to get the picture? Can you start to appreciate how invulnerable you are to the common slings and arrows of outrageous fortune?

Perhaps the most important aspect of all is psychological. Have you ever noticed how many businessmen these days appear in absolute agony? Sometimes it manifests itself as open hostility and other times it's just a case of I couldn't care less. Probably the most important measure of what you do for a living is how you feel about the day ahead when you first wake up in the morning. I've never found anything in my life that even comes close to the thrill of knowing I'll be surrounded by books and book lovers all day and be well paid for the privilege. It's a tough habit to break. I've seen many a septegenarian still going strong, though they're usually content to stay home and be mail-order booksellers by the time they get to be octogenarians.

BENEFITS AND BONUSES

Books are not absolutely dead things, but do contain a potency of life in them to be as active as that soul was whose progeny they are; nay they do preserve as in a vial the purest efficacy and extraction of that living intellect that bred them.

As good almost kill a man as kill a good book: who kills a man kills a reasonable creature, God's image; but he who destroys a good book kills reason itself.

A good book is the precious lifeblood of a master spirit, em balmed and treasured up on purpose to a life beyond life.

Milton

The pride and universal appeal of this profession, and I use the term profession advisedly, is easily understood. To many, books are the staff of life — friends which never fail. Books remember the eternal verities and are always there to refresh our memories. They have the power to bring a fever pitch of excitement to the most banal of lives. A bookseller's coin of the realm is man's most noble achievement — books!

The rewards are not all of the spirit, but corporal as well. Who among us has never nurtured fantasies of striking gold or of buried treasure? An antiquarian bookseller experiences that indescribable glow every time he reaches out to pluck that special book from a box he thought at first contained only general stock. When he checks its points in his reference and finds it's listed as scarce and valued at hundreds of dollars, he knows the same thrill as any treasure hunter who ever harvested a coin from the sea. This is as good a place as any to explain that I find it unwieldy to write ''his or her'' every time a personal pronoun is needed so I have been forced to compromise and have elected to consistently use the generic term ''he''. Rest assured I do so in the full knowledge that a great many of the antiquarian bookshops in the country are owned and operated by women, including some of the very best.

There are other aspects of this business which are just as gratifying in entirely different ways. For instance, there's that warm feeling of gratification as you hand that scarce book to a collector who's sought it in vain for years, fully aware he had no good reason to ever really expect to own it. Their gratitude is often very touching; you have given them something which transcends most material possessions. It may represent a vital link to their past, a long forgotten insight into a subject which fascinates, or it may fill a gap in some important collection. This is but one of the many wonderful bonuses which go along with the job.

During my years in the book business, I couldn't begin to estimate the numbers of people who confessed to having the dream of someday starting a shop of their own. It is the ultimate goal of countless book lovers of all ages.

As with so many things in life, it's easy when you know how. It really is incredibly simple, yet the path to success is narrow and the pitfalls many and often devastating. In this book I will show you how to avoid making any of those costly mistakes and launch a shop which will prosper in a remarkably brief period of time.

It is hardly necessary to go into those benefits which accrue to the owner of any small business, though they are considerable. Many of the unique bonuses are outlined to be covered in depth in later chapters. These include such things as tax-free travel, participating in book fairs and increasing or decreasing your income at will to minimize your tax liabilities.

An important bonus which should not be overlooked is the fact that a bookseller enjoys a rare and wonderful relationship with his peers, not just those in his city or town but those all over the world. When I had my shop in San Diego, never a day went by when I wasn't on the phone to other shops attempting to run down a particular title for one of my customers. Naturally the reverse was also true. I never hesitated to send a client to another store to buy a book. The thing they would always remember was that it was I who took the trouble to find the book for them. We sometimes got cards and letters of appreciation from these clients. Booksellers understand that if they work together to serve the public as best they can, everybody benefits. We even had maps printed giving brief descriptions of all the used shops in San Diego and clear directions on how to get there. It sounds a simple thing but stop and think what other industry operates that way. You think this extended family philosophy doesn't make life a lot more pleasant? You'd better know it does. I know we've all often yearned to see the whole world operate on just this kind of basis. I'm ashamed to have to say I don't believe any of us will ever live to see that happen, but, at least, in the community of antiquarian booksellers the respect and trust and understanding of our oneness is alive and well.

2
Qualifications for Success

Book love, my friends, is your pass to the greatest, the purest, and the most perfect pleasure that God has prepared for his creatures. It lasts when all other pleasures fade. It will support you when all other recreations are gone. It will last until your death. It will make your hours pleasant to you as long as you live.

Anthony Trollope

Just on the off chance you neglected to earn a Ph.D. in literature or library sciences, don't worry about it. So did I, along with just about everybody else who's successful in this business. It probably wouldn't have helped all that much if you had. More to the point, see whether or not you can honestly answer in the affirmative to the following questions:

Are you an avid reader? Do you have a deep and abiding love of books? Are your communicative skills reasonably good? Can you accept the idea of beginning a lifelong learning process which will never even be close to completed?

If you squeaked by with a yes to all of the above then you're a candidate. I didn't pose the question of honesty above. It didn't strike me as necessary. I'm operating on the premise that anyone who was interested enough to buy this book and can answer yes to the above prompts is scrupulously honest. If I'm wrong, do yourself a favor and go watch television because you'll never make it in this business. I don't believe in speaking in absolutes so I won't claim there isn't so much as a single rotten apple in the booksellers' barrel but there are damn few and I'd hate to think I was responsible for adding any. And please understand, when I speak of antiquarian booksellers I am referring to professionals with fine shops. I do not include antique stores or flea markets or other such places which may offer a number of books along with their other wares.

The entire industry is predicated on trust; it could never function as effectively as it does without it. All mail-order transactions are made sight unseen, remember. Dealers send checks often for thousands to dealers they've never met for books they've never seen. That's one of the truly beautiful things about this business. The wrong sort of individual just doesn't seem attracted to it. It is my theory that it's well nigh impossible to be a heavy reader without evolving a pretty strong set of moral values. How fine that makes it for those of us who elect to spend our lives within the bookselling community.

Don't get me wrong: if your I.Q. and your waist size are approximately the same you're either too dumb or too fat to make it as a bookman. But as long as you can lay claim to average intelligence coupled with a thirst for knowledge you'll do fine. It should comfort you to know there is such an incredible mass of material involved that no one dealer knows more than some tiny fraction of the whole. You never will either and that's OK. It's a little like being a doctor in general practice. He'll never know nearly enough either but as the years go by he'll have to look up less and less in his references. (You have one advantage over him; you won't have to hide from the client while you're looking things up. He does!)

Certainly it helps to have a somewhat retentive mind. Mine is more on the order of a sieve, which is what prompted me to place the following sign on my office wall. ''Everyone makes mistakes, but it would be more to your credit if you were to make different ones each time.''

When referring to references and the masses of material above, bear in mind this only has to do with the scarce and rare collectable portion of your shop and that's going to represent only a very little of your business in the beginning. Less than 5 per cent, surely. That's an interest some of us are drawn to and some of us aren't. It's entirely possible you may be satisfied to not get involved with rare books at all, content to wholesale off to a specialist dealer those that come your way by happenstance. In that case you can forget about masses of material because you can operate a lovely, highly profitable general stock shop in no time with your eyes closed.

There is a certain amount of physical vitality required, certainly. A busy shop will take in and put out a minimum of five hundred books per day. Putting them out's easy: clients bring them to the counter, pay you the money, and carry them out the door. But you have to take in as many as you put out or your stock is being depleted. That means at least five hundred books have to be shelved. The hardbacks have to be priced first. They not only have to be shelved, they have to be shelved in alphabetical order within the proper subject section. This is not much of a feat really, but it goes on every day and represents at least an hour of brisk effort. If it is a problem due to physical infirmity any young eager beaver can do it and young people love to work in bookstores.

FINANCIAL START-UP COSTS

A vital requirement to get your shop off and running is, of course, money. Filthy lucre! But don't panic; it's going to be a lot less than you anticipate. But there is an ante in the game and you'll have to be prepared to make it. One would think costs would vary widely from one section of the country to another but my experience in Southern California and the Ozarks of Missouri hasn't really born that out. So the figures given here should be valid within a fairly narrow range of variation.

In Chapter 4, I'll explain why it is wise to open your shop with relatively few books, but you will need some. I started with ten thousand, which may sound like a lot but it's really not. The world is full of used books. Admittedly most of them are of no value even as general stock but acquiring ten thousand over a period of a couple of months should be simple enough. I frankly hate garage sales but the one time I do go is when I'm building stock for a new store. If you come across a decent buy, make an offer for the entire lot. Never pay over 15 per cent of the original cover price for paperbacks and only buy them if they are in as new condition or very close to it. Hardbacks should be in dust wrappers, especially if they are novels. Be hesitant to pay much more than a quarter for book club novels. You'll find out how to recognize them later on. Publishers' editions are worth double that but only if it's an author you recognize or classic literature. Good nonfiction requires common sense. If I tell you to pay no more than a dollar you might pass up some beautiful art books worth twenty-five to fifty dollars. Again, subsequent chapters will provide you with some helpful guidelines.

Resist the urge to buy books simply because they are there. The majority of books are a very real liability, a fact that escapes all too many would-be-booksellers. Library sales are common throughout the country and nearly always worth while. The best I've ever attended is the annual sale held in Chicago as a fundraiser for Brandeis University in Chicago where they commonly offer in the neighborhood of one million books for sale. Such sales are often a treasure trove of older reference books which mean little to the reading public but are pure gold for the bookseller. The age of a price guide such as American Book Prices Current or Bookman's Price Index isn't important. The major reason you'll need these is for the points (the unique features which tell you whether or not the book you have in hand is indeed a first edition.).

Chapter 6 will go into specific detail concerning the kinds of books you should be acquiring. Locality will dictate a good deal, of course. Regional Americana is an absolute must but there may well be other patterns not quite so obvious.

For instance, Southern California is very big on science fiction/fantasy, while the Ozarks is more into historical romances and westerns. This is the sort of input which may be easily gained from local new book stores. Simply observing the amount of space allotted to the various catagories will tell you a great deal.

Most of the ten thousand odd volumes I begin a store with are brought to me. I accomplish this by the simple expedient of running an ad in the local throwaway paper. By throwaway newspaper I refer to the free periodical to be found in most cities of any size, usually called something on the order of *Penny Power* or *Penny Saver* or whatever. For some reason these journals really produce results when you're offering to spend money. A typical ad of mine would read: ''Top prices paid for your clean hardback and paperback books.'' Prepare to be very, very busy. It's just that simple. If your town doesn't have one of these free weekly papers, I'm sure the local newspaper will serve as well. The total cost for the ten thousand volumes I bought in this manner prior to opening my last shop was twenty-eight hundred dollars. They were approximately 40 per cent hardbacks, many brand new, and 60 per cent paperbacks. That was my total outlay for opening stock for a business which was netting me four thousand dollars per month by the fourth month of operation. And the business didn't owe anybody a dime. It's definitely a retailer's dream come true.

The next expenditure you will have will be the lease of a building. Please note I did say lease. Never start a business with a month-to-month tenancy.

More details in Chapter 3 concerning leases. Some landlords will require a first and last month's rent. It's hard to put hard dollar amounts down here because of the wide spread of rental costs throughout the country. In San Diego I paid one thousand dollars a month rent for an inferior location and an old building with a leaky roof. In Springfield I paid seven hundred dollars per month for a larger space in a brand new building in a nice shopping center. So let's arbitrarily set aside another two thousand dollars for the purpose of obtaining a lease.

Now you have to estimate the amount of materials needed to construct your beautiful shop. Chapter 5 should guide you through this, the most physically demanding part of your career as a bookseller. The sum total of all my materials for my most recent shop, including everything, was just over twenty-two hundred dollars. I was fortunate in that, since the building was new, the carpeting was good and no interior painting was required. The money went for shelving lumber, wood and formica for the checkout stand, used cash register, desk calculator and a little 1.7 cubic foot refrigerator for food and cold drinks.

That totals seven thousand dollars and we're almost there. All that's left is city and county business licenses — something on the order of ten dollars each. Security deposit to the utility company if you haven't had a business account before. This is commonly double your highest estimated monthly total bill. This amounted to two hundred and fifty dollars in my case but would vary greatly due to climate and utility rates in your area. Some phone companies also require a security deposit, though I have never run into it personally. Last stop with your checkbook in hand should be the office of your State Franchise Tax Board. You're going to have to obtain a Retail Sales Permit and tax number. You are about to become an unpaid employee of the state in the sense that you will be collecting sales tax on all but your wholesale transactions. The state anticipates that you will turn over that sales tax to them on a monthly or quarterly basis. To insure that you do so, they will ask you to post a bond or take out a certificate of deposit in both your name and theirs and let them hold it until such time as you surrender your tax permit. To post a bond is quite inexpensive but, if you can spare a few hundred dollars, it's better to buy a certificate of deposit and let the state hold it. That way it not only doesn't cost you anything, you're collecting interest on the C.D.

The only other possible expense I can conjure up is the cost of filing for a fictitious name which is required in some states when you start a business under a name other than your own. This runs about thirty-five dollars.

Your name and the name of all principals in the proposed business along with the name you've selected for your shop is listed in the local business/legal newspaper, giving any past creditors or those with the same business name a chance to contest your filing.

So there you have it; a very close estimate which takes you right up to the day you hang out your *OPEN sign*. You've spent less than eight thousand dollars so far, but your shelves are looking pretty empty. That's just the way you want it. An in-depth explanation of what comes next will be found in Chapter 4 but for now, let me assure you that it's going to cost you very little to stock those shelves. Something on the order of 80 per cent of the books you'll acquire once you're open will cost you nothing! You'll trade for them. And every time you trade you double that portion of your stock free. Since you'll offer double the value in trade credit as you will in cash, about the only ones who'll want to sell instead of trade are those moving away and those who aren't interested in books but have acquired some somehow.

My records show I spent an additional three thousand dollars during the first two months after opening for the acquisition of books. But by then the money to buy these books was being generated by the business, no longer money out of pocket. And after the first two months, as the shelves filled, the amount of money spent on books dropped rapidly.

I think it would be prudent to allocate the total sum of fifteen thousand dollars to the launching of a really fine previously-owned book shop. This will give you a comfortable cushion and allow you to sleep better at night. There will inevitably be tension and uncertainty until such a project is underway and the principals are able to see that it really does all work and the income is there. An extra few thousand in the company coffers will provide that little edge of self-confidence which will mean a lot. If it occurs to you that there must be lots of other expenses such as advertising, relax. Chapter 7 will explain why this doesn't hold true for the antiquarian book business.

LONG-TERM GOALS

The majority of used book shop owners are satisfied to plug along making more money than the average attorney, never displaying at book fairs or printing catalogues, content with keeping their stores clean and well-stocked. God bless; there's not a thing in the world wrong with that. But there are others of us who will be driven, usually by personal interest, to become more and more expert in one of the myriad aspects of the antiquarian book business. The rewards are great and the possibilities nearly endless. It's more like living out a childhood fantasy than it is working.

Dozens of dealers specialize in ephemera exclusively. In 1984, a telegram from General Eisenhower, signed, brought twenty-three thousand five hundred dollars at auction, just to give you an idea how valuable comparatively contemporary paper items can be. There are a surprising number of dealers who specialize in children's literature. What could be more fun! And the market is very active. Wait until you visit your first book fair and see those little, delicate nineteenth century books of only a few dozen pages locked under glass with price tags in the hundreds of dollars. Then there are the holographic specialists who deal only in autographs, TLS's (typed letter signed) and any hand-written material. Here again, the market is brisk. The most outstanding example which comes to mind is the auctioning off a few years ago of a holographic treatise in the hand of Da Vinci. American oil mogul, Armand Hammer, bought it at auction for something in excess of ten million dollars. Interestingly enough, the book was placed in auction by a London bookseller who found it among a lot of rather ordinary books when he was called to come and clean out the books from the attic of an elderly woman. He paid one hundred pounds for the entire lot.

The list of specialities is a long one; you may be the one to make it even longer. I've seen specialists in medical books, law, physical culture, philosophy of science, spelunking, aviation, sailing and theater, just for a few examples. This doesn't mean you can open a shop in Fort Dodge, Iowa and operate a successful shop handling nothing but books on Haiku. Specialty shops require either a large metropolitan setting or a sophisticated mail-order operation. But as you spend time in this business, your natural tendency will be to specialize and you will build up a quality mailing list because dealers and collectors will visit you and implore you to quote appropriate material to them. You'll be running lists of books for sale in the weekly trade journal known as the *Antiquarian Bookman* and you'll keep records of regular buyers in order to quote to them directly. It's natural to indulge your own interests if you do give in to this urge to specialize, but you must marry up your interests with those of your clients as well. When I had a shop in Southern California it worked very well because I have an interest in science fiction. Years later when I opened a store in the Ozarks it didn't work as well so I slanted my specialized stock more toward illustrated books and local history. Indulge yourself by all means — that's half the fun — but serve your customers' needs while you're at it.

Let me give you an example of what typically happens when you start a used book store. I'll use the history of a nice shop in Colorado Springs that recently celebrated its twenty-fifth anniversary in business. They opened with about the size shop I'll be describing in detail in the following chapter. The man and wife proprietors earned a good living and dreamed of the day their store would do a hundred thousand dollars annual gross. They served their public well, maintained a clean, attractive shop, and today they are grossing over two million annually. Nothing spectacular happened along the way; it's just natural in this business for every day to be a little bit better than the day before. You are constantly upgrading your stock so your sales increase. You are routinely providing an almost unheard of service in this day and age so your customer count climbs constantly. It's hard to describe the personal bond which develops between you and many of your regulars. It's totally unlike any retail customer/owner relationship I can think of. The nearest example which comes to mind, oddly enough, is that between patient and the archetypal old family physician. There is more about the business that is old and unique than just the books. There are values and personal relationships and business associations that are rarely to be found today.

Under this heading of long term goals, I feel compelled to tell you that the antiquarian book business is a very management-intensive one. I've seen owners reach a very comfortable level of income within a very short time, then decide to make their shops into a latch-key operation and hire clerks, usually for minimum, and retire. It doesn't work that way. If you aren't committed to the idea of being there personally much of the time, I respectfully suggest perhaps this isn't the business for you.

It's not that there's anything very difficult about the day-to-day operation of a shop — there isn't — but a hundred little decisions have to be made every day and each is important in its own way. You can't put a clerk behind the desk unless you empower him or her to make those decisions. The chances of you finding someone involved enough to do that satisfactorily are long indeed. I've had some wonderful assistants in my shops. I've been able to leave on vacations, book fairs and buying trips without a qualm. But I only hire professionals with background and training as antiquarian booksellers. I pay them well and I pay them commissions. Chapter 11 covers this in detail but let me make the point here and now. It will cost you a great deal of money to hire someone who's only capable of working the adding machine and making change. Wait until you can afford it and then hire someone *Good* and give them plenty of incentive to *Sell.* It's the soundest investment you'll ever make.

3

There's No Such Thing
As a Perfect Location

(But There Are a
Hell of a Lot
of Bad Ones)

WHAT TO LOOK FOR IN A SITE

There was a time in this business when the popular wisdom was to find the weirdest and least expensive spot possible to set up your shop. Convert an old house, find a walk-up nobody else wanted, anything as long as it was cheap enough. The myth was that die-hard bookaholics would seek you out anywhere and, perhaps in the tradition of *The Old Curiosity Shop*, the stranger the atmosphere the better your customers would like it. It's no doubt true the die-hards will seek you out if you locate beneath a bridge, but unless you wish to embrace a vow of poverty you'd better disregard the above premise entirely. It went out with iceboxes and button shoes.

There are going to be literally dozens of times within this book when I will advise you not to spend your money but this will be one exception. If ever in your life you're going to play Diamond Jim Brady, let this be it. Low rent is nearly always the poorest bargain possible. You're going to expend just as much blood, sweat and tears in a bad location as you will in a good one. The only difference is you won't make the money you deserve in the former. Trust me; penny wise and pound foolish is the byword when it comes to rent. I've seen too many dealers isolate themselves from the public in cul-de-sacs and low traffic areas with the inevitable results. Either their business dies a slow lingering death or, at best, they peddle their life's blood — which is time — for a pittance.

The following parameters are vital. Your chosen location should encompass most of them certainly and hopefully all of them. This is the first and perhaps the most important decision that will determine your economic future. The qualities you need are:

Frontage on a street with a very high traffic count.

Plenty of off-street parking.

Good section of town where people of all ages are comfortable coming to shop.

Store front easily visible from the street. (Or at least compensating permanent sign space included in the lease.)

A minimum area of sixteen hundred square feet including a small back room and toilet facilities.

Your best bet is a shopping center with a heavy anchor. An anchor is any major chain store which attracts vast multitudes of warm bodies such as Sears, Safeway, K Mart or any of a host of others. Or it could be a very successful local operation, as long as there is a heavy traffic flow of people around your shop during the hours you intend to be open. For example, a big theater complex may draw multitudes but won't do you much good if they don't have matinees.

At the same time you must avoid locating in a center where parking is too far removed from your shop. The nice enclosed malls you see popping up all around the country won't work for you. Remember your customers have to be capable of lugging heavy boxes and bags of books to and from your store conveniently.

Impulse buying, as any experienced retailer knows, makes up a very large portion of every store's volume. Your shop will be no exception. Think of it as a simple mathematical equation, which indeed it is. For every one hundred people exposed to your store and the stock therein, X volume of dollars results. Believe me, it's an entirely valid premise. So be darn sure you locate where you'll harvest lots of X's.

There is a tendency today to build a lot of cutesy little shops in tourist-trap areas, along the beach or in the old section of town or wherever the local attraction is in your town. These shops are usually outrageously expensive, which is fine because they are inappropriate for you anyway. Tourists are never going to be much help to you, other than dealers on buying trips. Study the shopping patterns within your community and place yourself where the basic, heavyweight retailers are. Stay away from centers made up of funky little off-the-wall shops where they're fortunate to see two dozen customers a day. A major grocery store would be my first choice but one of the big variety stores such as Wards or Walmart is just as good. You can bet a lot of money was spent by these stores before they chose their location so why not take advantage of their wisdom?

There are other, more subtle reasons for paying the extra freight to locate in a really good area. One is the fact that judgments will be made concerning you and your business every day based upon your address. When one of the local bibliophiles passes on to that big library in the sky, who do you think the heirs are going to call to come and buy his library? You may be certain it won't be the guy who's situated in the low rent district. The only way people who are not familiar with any of the shops personally have of judging you is by your location. It's a constant message you're sending out to the world: I'm a class act. It's long been a custom of businessmen such as real estate brokers and insurance brokers and others to make certain they live in the most prestigious section of town. Frankly I find that laughable but in the case of an antiquarian book shop it is advisable.

I don't want to overstate the case. Please don't think you have to be in the absolute best center in town or forget the whole thing. We all have to do the best we can from what's available at the time. And there are even centers that are *too* posh. I remember one such center in La Jolla, California, where there were only stores like Saks, expensive jewelry stores and furriers. I'm convinced a used book shop there would have been a major mistake. The people who patronized those shops wouldn't dream of going into a used anything store. If they did it would be like a duchess darting into a hock shop. So look for a stable, busy location with all of the qualities mentioned at the beginning of this chapter. It won't be difficult to find, at least in most cities. As you read on you'll get a clearer picture of what's ideal and the reasons why. But it's hardly my intention that everyone who starts a shop using this book as a guide will end up with a carbon copy of my shops. Of course you won't. Your town will dictate what is and what isn't available; your own personality will alter the way in which you implement the suggestions herein.

THOUGHTS ON NEGOTIATING A LEASE

This is an area where the variation in prevailing conditions is apt to be greater than any other subject covered in this book. Some will find themselves negotiating with a kindhearted owner of a small building, while others will be faced with dealing with an agent from a management firm which takes care of a shopping center owned by a holding company in another state. Needless to say, the former is more likely to gain concessions but not always. I've found the world to be full of wonderful people and some of them even work for big, faceless corporations.

Rule number one is *always* sign a lease. There are no exceptions. The minimum should be three years. Five is better.

Next rule is to get an option for the same amount of time as the original lease. It's a thousand times easier to negotiate an additional option at the time you arrange for your lease than it will be down the road a couple of years as your lease runs short. Always negotiate from as much of a position of power as possible. Most of the power is with the landlord, assuming he has a successful building, so utilize what little you have when you have it. (And if he doesn't have a successful building, what are you doing dealing with him anyway?)

I know it's a little frightening the first time you sign a long-term lease and realize — sink or swim — you're obligated for the total rent during the entire duration of the lease. Like anything else, it gets easier with practice. You're not really sticking your neck out as much as you might think. If you do move for any reason before the lease is up, the worst thing that can happen is you'll have to pay the rent until the landlord gets another tenant. If you've selected wisely there's only one reason why you'd want to move and that is you're so successful you need more room. In that case you'll be so flush you won't mind paying the rent for a month or two after you move; it shouldn't take any longer than that to re-rent it if it's a suitable spot. But even that isn't common. Your location becomes more and more valuable to you with every passing month so the idea is to select well, build with class and stay put. You can grow later on by upgrading the quality of your stock without increasing your square footage.

Just to reinforce the dictum about never operating without a lease, let me tell you a story about a fine young lady I know who bought an antiquarian book shop that was already established. The individual she bought it from had never had a lease, never wanted one because she thought it was safer that way. She passed this impression on to my friend who accepted it and continued operating her shop on a month-to-month rental agreement. All was well for a couple of years; her shop prospered and she was delighted. Then she went away on vacation for a few weeks. When she returned and began going through her accumulated mail she found an eviction notice from her landlord. It seems the business next door to her wanted to expand and had offered to sign a lease for her shop. Naturally the landlord wanted the security of a lease, given a choice. When he couldn't contact her to see if she would have been willing to sign a lease, he made a prudent business decision and gave a lease to the neighboring business. So there she was, faced with less than two weeks to dismantle what was a successful business and get out. It was a real tragedy because she depended on the income from that shop to support herself and in fact she was still making payments on the business to the person she bought it from. I think you can see how foolish it would be for you to ever allow yourself to be in such a vulnerable position. It's about as dumb as building a luxurious home on land you don't own and then wondering why someone came along and took it away from you. That happened to a friend of mine, too, in Baja California, Mexico. 'Nough said? Get a lease plus an option for the same term as the lease.

The option will be for slightly more money, of course. You can't expect to pay the same rent year after year. But it's important to negotiate the option rent right at the beginning. There's a trend these days for the big shopping center owners to demand what is known as a triple-net lease. In its simplest terms, this means your rent is increased at whatever intervals the lease states, based upon an often complicated formula using any number of data sources. The most common is the United States Bureau of Labor and Statistics published rate of inflation which comes out monthly. During the high inflation days in the late 1970s I watched too many thriving businesses go under due to this outrageous system to ever suggest anyone submit to it. With the inflation rate as low as it is as I write this it seems harmless enough but the pendulum swings both ways. I know a book shop in Southern California that saw its rent go from eight hundred dollars a month to twelve hundred dollars a month between 1977 and 1979 due to this system of triple-net. And it doesn't end there. (Why do you think they call it triple-net?) Not only do you indemnify the landlord against inflation, you also have to reimburse him for any increase in his insurance or in his property taxes. Triple-net leases are unfair and dangerous for the lessee. Avoid them at all costs. If it means opting for a somewhat less desirable location in order to get a straightforward lease, I'd advise you to do so. Signing a triple-net is a lot like handing your credit card to an irresponsible friend and hoping for the best.

I'm sure it won't work every time but here are a couple of very helpful thoughts on using your power when negotiating a lease. I once got a landlord to give me the six weeks I needed to build the interior of the shop free, starting the rent only on the day I opened the door for business. Another time I got a landlord who wanted nine hundred dollars a month to give me a chance to grow up to it. He accepted seven hundred the first year, eight hundred the second year, and got his nine hundred during the third year. The store was easily worth the nine hundred he was asking but, as with most people in the world, he was a nice guy. People love to feel good about themselves and very often all you have to do is ask and give them that chance to do you a favor. I've been on both sides of the desk. I've owned and leased houses, stores and warehouses. If I felt I was dealing with someone who was reliable, energetic and motivated to be successful, I'd do anything within reason to help them succeed. If you present yourself in this way you'll be surprised how accommodating people will be. One the other hand, if you find yourself poised across the desk from a real bastard, it's time to re-evaluate. There's no reason to walk away from a deal just because the landlord or his representative has the personality of a Malthusian swamp rat. You don't need him for a friend and once the lease is signed you'll probably never see him again anyway. But if it comes down to a choice between two locations, interview both landlords. It may make the decision for you.

After you've found your space, give it a very close inspection. It's easy to get little things taken care of, or at least promised, before you sign the lease. Afterward it may get a whole lot harder. You are going to be responsible for the upkeep of the interior, it's true, but you have every right to expect to start out with a clean, unblemished shop where everything works. But it's up to you to search out any flaws and point them out.

This may sound redundant but read the lease very carefully. Don't just casually check to see that the figures are right and accept the landlord's statement that it's just the standard form. They have a habit of being most meticulous about spelling out all of your obligations in great detail but they sometimes neglect to elucidate their own quite as clearly. The landlord has certain obligations and you're well advised to make damn sure the lease spells them out. Where does it say he must maintain the roof? Is it in there that the exterior is to be clean and freshly painted at all times? How often is the parking lot to be swept? How much snow has to accumulate before he's obligated to have it plowed? These are all items which properly belong in your lease. If they're not the first time around, don't panic. It doesn't make him a bad guy. He's just an experienced businessman looking out for number one and the more strongly he can structure the lease in his favor the better from his standpoint. It's up to you to look out for yourself in these affairs. Never hesitate to point something like this out to him; he'll only respect you for it and that's something you want to achieve.

LONG-TERM CONSIDERATIONS

After the initial terror goes away — as I recall it only lasts a few weeks — and you accept the fact that everything really is going to be fine, then comes a glorious honeymoon era between you and your lovely new business. The danger lurks somewhere around eighteen months or two years down the road. It always happens and it's insidious. Your customers keep asking you why you don't carry _____. (You fill in the blank. It usually consists of things like old magazines, comic books, old post cards, you name it and somebody will ask you for it eventually.) Suddenly you're going to begin having visions of a shop of twice the size where you never have to disappoint anyone. If the new shop is twice the size, of course you're going to make twice the profit — right? Maybe!

One thing you don't want to do is open a second shop. The only exception I can possibly think of is if you're in business with a family member or a very close friend and you're both capable of running a shop. Otherwise, opening another location accomplishes several things — all bad. It detracts from your original store because you aren't going to be there as much and presumably you are the store's principal asset. It also increases your overhead by more than double because your payroll in the new shop is going to be far more than it was at the first location. Some of the increase you'll pick up in the second store will be offset by a slowing of growth at the first. The Tsar of the Book World Complex affects most of us and it's often a setback instead of a coup. Multiple locations just don't seem to work out well at all.

The happiest growth formula I've seen work is when an adjacent store becomes vacant and all you have to do is punch an opening in the wall and you're in business. This is ideal because the added rent is really the only ongoing increase in your cost of doing business. You shouldn't even need any added staff. Stock is no problem because you're turning away loads of books every day; now all you have to do is start accepting more in trade until the new half is stocked. You leave the door to the new half locked so the traffic is all by your desk; therefore the combined shops may still be operated by one person.

Moving to a larger shop is all right too, but the closer to the old one the better. I've always been put off by the sheer enormity of the job of moving an entire book store and having to build all those miles of shelving all over again. But if you're young and eager enough, there's no real reason not to. My personal opinion is that you can accomplish the same thing without all the perspiration by simply upgrading your original shop but just as many do it the other way and it works. Perhaps you never really do get intrigued with the scarcer collectable material and you just want to have more room for general stock. Nothing in the world wrong with that. Your location in the country will necessarily have a good deal to do with which way you jump, too. One good reason in favor of relocating is in the event you find yourself in an economically declining area of your city. This is bad now and will be critical when the time comes for you to sell your business.

Let me give you one more tidbit of advice to remember if and when you ever do expand. Stay away from newspapers and magazines. If you don't know better you might easily get the notion from some of your customers' comments that old magazines would really go. And you keep turning them down for trade so obviously getting them isn't going to be a problem. Let me tell you what it's like being in the used periodical business. You have absolutely no idea how many hundreds of thousands of magazines you'd have to stock to have any chance at all of having what any given client wants. So you stock a thousand magazines just so you'll have the right one and then they'll howl like a wounded banshee and tell you you've got a nerve charging them ten dollars for an old copy of whatever. On top of that, old magazines don't bear up well under handling and are extremely difficult to display. About the only thing you can do in the end is stack them and then the covers quickly become detached as they are pulled from the stack. You end up throwing out many times more than you'll ever sell. It's a heartbreaking, thankless task and you're well advised to spare yourself the aggravation. I've seen it tried many times and I've yet to see it work satisfactorily except by mail-order. There was a fine attempt to establish such a shop in San Diego in 1978. It was called Paper Antiquities and the owner knew what he was doing and I think he did everything as well as it could be done. It didn't fly.

I'll qualify the above remarks by stating that I welcome bound newspapers and magazines on my shelves. They are common in library bindings and pre-1920 they are often bound in full calf and can be quite lovely. As libraries transfer material to microfilm these bound periodicals are turning up and are well worth the shelf space they require.

4

You Say You Don't Happen to Have Fifty Thousand Books Lying Around?

You despise books; you whose whole lives are absorbed in the vanities of ambition, the pursuit of pleasure, or in indolence; but remember that all the known world, excepting only savage nations, is governed by books.

Voltaire

ACQUIRING YOUR OPENING STOCK

Yes, fifty thousand; it will take just about that many books to stock the minimum sixteen hundred square foot shop described within this book. And what makes it a lot tougher is we're talking about fifty thousand interesting books in fine condition — in other words: saleable books.

No doubt this is one of the things which concerns you most. If so, relax! It's easier than you think. The world is chock full of books. Even taking into consideration the very real fact that the majority are junk either by reason of content or condition there are still many times what you need out there waiting for you.

You must first learn to avoid trash in your fervor to build up an opening stock. So many books are liabilities, not assets. A few examples are: textbooks, Reader's Digest Condensed Books, old Harlequins, Gothics, books on political science, sociology, economics and most book club novels.

Detailed discussion of this subject may be found in Chapter 9 but the above-mentioned are some of the types of books you'll come upon constantly and the sooner you learn to never let them clutter up your shelves the better.

The more lead time you allow yourself the less it will cost you to stock your store. If you're in a rush it's not difficult to stock a fine book shop within a three month period. I've done it more than once. All you have to do is run an ad in your local paper. Even better, your town probably has one of those free classified weeklies, usually called something inane like *Penny Power or Penny Pincher.* These are very effective when you're offering people money for something they never expected to be able to convert to cash. Word your ad something like this: '' *Books Wanted!!* Top prices paid for your clean hardback and paperbacks. Most subjects (Phone number.)''

Now stand back and try to avoid being trampled in the rush. I picked up over ten thousand books within a month that way when I opened my latest store in 1984. I know it sounds like one hell of a lot of books but it's amazing how they disappeared once they were on the shelves. When they were shelved the store still looked empty.

But that's exactly how you want it. The idea isn't to go chasing all over the countryside paying out hard cash for books. All you want or need is a small nucleus of stock when you open your doors in order to begin trading with your customers. Wonder of wonders, you are going to fill up all those empty shelves free for the most part. Your customers are going to bring them to you and be enormously grateful for the privilege. That new shop where they bought them certainly doesn't want them back; if not for you their only other option would be the agony of a garage sale.

Trading books works pretty much the same from coast to coast; we'll cover that completely in Chapter 8. Suffice it to say, trading is the best thing that ever evolved within the antiquarian book industry. I mean that from the standpoint of the consumer as well as that of the shop owner. The principle is simplicity itself — you always trade two for one. Two hardbound books gets the client one new one. Two paperbacks gets him one new title. It's a terrific customer service and the principal way in which you acquire your stock. For the buyer, it certainly beats trading with a friend who might be able to offer a few dozen titles which the buyer has probably either already read or isn't the least bit interested in. Put yourself in his shoes and imagine his delight at being able to turn in all of his old books —

at least the clean, sharp ones — and select from tens of thousands of new, unread titles all beautifully displayed in a pleasant shop. It's little wonder your clients appreciate you. They rarely get such a fair shake from any retailer.

Your side of the coin isn't too shabby either. Every time you trade two for one *You double that portion of your stock absolutely free.* Soon after opening you'll find yourself trading hundreds of books daily. In no time at all those shelves will fill and you'll find you can keep them that way while spending very little, even as the money comes rolling in. It's one of life's rare, perfect exchanges wherein both parties benefit and there is no victim.

Just about the only time you'll be expending any meaningful amount of cash for books is when you are offered a fine library, usually upon the demise of the collector. Such opportunities are exciting when the offering is a quality one. It means a trip away from the shop usually. I won't go to someone's home to look at books unless there are at least several hundred hardbacks or the books described sound exceptional such as literary sets bound in full calf. I'd estimate I turn down three out of four libraries I'm invited out to see. All too often you arrive to find nothing but book club novels or Reader's Digests, old textbooks, books suffering the ravages of mildew. People who aren't really into books don't seem to know the difference between a book in fine condition and a throw-away. You qualify them over the phone, of course, and they'll tell you the books are wonderful — just like new. Then you arrive and find nothing but chipped spines, cracked hinges and not a dust wrapper in the lot. But hang in there because that fourth call is going to make your day. I've had some that made my year. Until it happens to you, you'll never know the thrill of walking into a room walled solid with big, beautiful Abram's art books or row upon row of rich leatherbounds. When discussing advertising in Chapter 7 I'll show you how to ensure that you'll be offered such prizes when they come available.

NEVER STOCK UNSALEABLE BOOKS MERELY BECAUSE THEY'RE AVAILABLE AND CHEAP

You will have to resist the wild urge to see those shelves filled as soon as possible after opening. It's true you want books, tens of thousands of books, but remember every bad book you shelve will cost you money. It's also true no two dealers would entirely agree on what constitutes a bad book but there are certain universal verities we may depend upon.

Learn to judge the value and desirability of any given book first of all by its condition. If it fails that test it doesn't much matter what the material is. One of the most common mistakes dealers make is to place ratty-looking books on display, thus downgrading the appearance of their shops. Chipped spines look terrible on the shelf and should never be tolerated unless the book is at least early nineteenth century and the content important.

Cracked hinges and badly shaken books (books where the pages are no longer tightly bound to the cover) fall into the same category. You must make allowances for the passing years but certainly there is no excuse for stocking a contemporary book with either of these shortcomings. In Chapter 12 we'll get into simple repairs which may be accomplished to overcome both of the above defects but the book would have to be of some merit to justify the time required.

Some books you will want to reject before you even look at them. The sickly smell of mildew will hit you as soon as you open the box or bag. Mildew may not be the problem in many parts of the country it is here in the Midwest, but mildew is a fungus and it does spread so you don't want infected books on your shelves.

I've even rejected lots of books because they stank heavily of tobacco smoke. (It's usually western paperbacks for some reason.) People are getting more and more militant about smokers these days and rightfully so. According to the latest Surgeon General's Report, secondary smoke (the effects suffered by non-smokers in the presence of smokers.) is far more damaging than most would have believed. It's not much different for a smoker to light up in your presence than it would be for him to add a minute pinch of poison to your food. It's stupid and indefensible. I merely bring this up so that you'll understand that a no smoking policy in your shop is advisable. I'm tempted to use a stronger word, such as absolutely necessary, but there are still a good many successful shops which do allow smoking so I'll resist the urge to let my own strong feelings on the subject spill over onto the page.

I cannot over-emphasize the importance of dust wrappers. If a book was issued with a dust jacket, and nearly all were during this century, it should be present. Think about it: there are only two ways of knowing the contents of any given book. One is to read the book and the other is to read the panels on the inside of the jacket. Certainly a collectable first edition without its wrapper is of no interest to any collector and is of little more value than a reading copy. Dust wrappers sell books. They look great on the shelf. They're designed by experts in the field to attract the eye and the copy they contain is designed to make the sale.

It would be a grave overstatement to say you must never accept any book which is missing its dust wrapper. There are many titles — principally non-fiction — which you'll be glad to have even without the jacket but it is always a regrettable flaw affecting both value and its saleability. The list of fiction which you will accept without jackets will be far briefer. These will consist primarily of classics (Hemingway, Faulkner, Twain, etc.) and a very few contemporary authors whose works you'll never have enough of. Names which come to mind are Michener, Wouk, Ludlum and King.

The point here is that you must establish right from the beginning the premise that you are not accepting just any old trash, that your shop is featuring a quality offering, and that anyone wishing to take advantage of your trade or purchase policy is going to have to play fair and bring you material of a like quality to that which they take out. Unfortunately, there will never come a time when you don't have to plow through offerings of junk and reject them but that becomes less and less common as your shop projects its image of quality. These things are always self-perpetuating. If you offer rough, uninteresting books, that's what people will bring you—the few who will even bother to come at all. If you run a class act you'll develop a class clientele who'll bring you like material. Think about it. You make certain judgments every time you walk into a retail store. You register details such as: is the store clean? Is the staff genuinely concerned with serving your needs? Is the stock being offered of good or poor quality? Is the pricing reasonable?

Your customers will do the same thing. They are not going to bring you their fine quality books in trade unless you are able to offer a like value in return. Learn to think of poor stock such as shabby books or unwrapped book club novels as the liabilities which they in fact are.

As with anything else, it gets easier with practice. You'll soon peer into a box or a bag and often that will be enough. If the books are dusty, damp or reek of mildew, there is no reason to examine them further.

All of the same principles apply to paperbacks, except of course they have no dust wrappers. Dog-eared pocket books will destroy the image it is so important that you project. There are some people who can read a paperback and it's garbage.

There's another flaw you must be on the lookout for and it applies to both paperbacks and hardbacks. Underlining or highlighting. There is a strange breed of reader who reads with a pencil, pen, or felt-tipped marker in his hand. When he finishes with a book it is trash. Have you ever tried to read a book which has been highlighted? It's most annoying and you certainly won't want to offer any such tomes on your shelves. Fortunately it isn't necessary to inspect every book you take in for this malady. Merely flip through the pages of the first several books. If you don't find any such defacing in the first few you can stop worrying about it. It is of course more common among nonfiction than it is with novels. Funny thing about it; the underlining never seems to extend much beyond the first few dozen pages. It's a phenomenon I've watched with interest for years. The obvious conclusion is that the mental midgets who so destroy their books never seem to be able to complete one. There are shops which are not concerned with this shortcoming but they are never quality stores. Some at least have the class to note inside the book the fact there is some underlining and adjust the price downward accordingly. That's a step in the right direction but better by far not to offer it at all unless it happens to be a several hundred year old beauty listed as scarce in the price guides. In that case, exceptions will be made, of course.

Avoid books with prices written in or on them in ink or wax pencil. Believe it or not there are shops where they actually destroy the value of the very books they are attempting to sell by defacing them in this way. Another foolish custom is to stick a piece of masking tape onto a book and write a price on that. This is a favorite ploy among the garage sale crowd. If the masking tape stays on for more than a couple of weeks it's going to damage the paperback's cover when it's removed. It's even worse on the dust wrapper of a hard back; it will leave an abrasion on all but the most glossy of paper even if it's pulled the next day. Besides which it's just too much trouble to bother with.

In certain cities I've run into the despicable custom of stamping prices in ink on paperbacks, usually on the bottom edges of the pages. Even more common is the custom of stamping the name and address of the shop inside the front cover of every book. The first thing it should tell you about a store is that they don't sell very many books or they wouldn't have the time for such foolishness. All of these and other similar customs are the mark of an amateur. No professional ever does anything to deface the product he sells. These sad examples of thoughtlessness are symptomatic of the negative — in some cases downright paranoid — attitudes to be found among those who operate along the fringe of the business. As do we all, they carry the seeds of their own destruction. But most of us are not quite so overt about our faults. Would you believe that I've actually seen stores where they price their paperbacks at half cover price, as is the usual custom, but *marked the price on every book in felt-tipped pen?* Maybe Freud could have explained it to me but no one else has been able to. The only logical explanation I can think of is the owner had such contempt for his customers he didn't believe they would be able to divide the publishers' prices in half. (Or perhaps he had trouble doing it.)

HOW TO SPIN YOUR WHEELS SEEKING YOUR INITIAL STOCK

When you're attempting to amass enough books to start your shop there may be a tendency to rush into foolish transactions. Some of the more common mistakes include buying thousands of paperbacks from other dealers. Even assuming they give you a great wholesale price, the odds are you're going to end up with marginal material at best. And you're vulnerable because you're ill-equipped to tell the difference as yet. It's all but a dead certainty you'll only be bailing him out of his mistakes so I don't recommend it. On the other hand, your fellow dealers are generally eager to help and very supportive of your efforts. I've bought heavily from dealers at times and there's nothing wrong with that *once you know what you're doing.* Until then it's strictly caveat emptor. I'd hate to think how many hundreds of hours I've no doubt wasted attending auction sales looking for books. The people who write up the ads for sales must be some of the most creative fiction writers in the world. Compare one of the lists in the paper with the actual material on hand and you'll see what I mean. There are certain key words which have been proven to draw. Antiques is one and it'll be a rare auction ad which doesn't offer antiques even if it only consists of a few old pieces of china and a washboard. Another is books. The word "books" in an ad pulls and there are nearly always at least some books in any given household. Better yet, if the books are a couple of decades old, they'll advertise "old books" or "antique books." (By the way, there is no such accepted nomenclature as "antique books.") This swells the crowd but it can make you crazy until you finally accept the fact that going to auction sales in search of marketable books is a complete waste of time.

Please understand the above refers to auctions of household items; it certainly does not reflect my views on book auctions. Book auctions are a delight and you will indeed be fortunate if you are located in a large metropolitan area where you'll have access to them. I've been known to travel a couple of thousand miles for no other reason than to attend an auction of scarce and rare books. It's probably good that I don't live in an area where they are common; I tend to run amok and buy everything in sight.

I briefly mentioned before that sections are self-perpetuating. This is absolutely true and it brings up one of the more difficult tasks you'll be faced with when initially building your stock. Let me give you an example: when I opened my most recent store in the Ozarks I had no trouble getting most of the kinds of books I wanted but I wasn't able to make any headway towards building the impressive illustrated section I desired. Finally I called the man back in Southern California who'd bought my last store and negotiated to buy some fifty fine Heritage illustrated books. These beauties are in slipcases and make a very nice display. As soon as they arrived and hit the shelf similar material began coming in, often to be used as trade value towards those very books. So however you can, you've got to "salt" the tough sections sometimes to get them rolling.

Book auctions are a good way of doing that if they are available to you. The problem is, it will be a while before you will be comfortable making the lightning-swift decisions required at an auction. I used to go with a more experienced bookseller and lean upon his expertise when I was starting out. Book auctions are like any auction: one time everything will bring higher than retail and the next everything will be given away.

We've touched upon garage sales lightly in an earlier chapter. They seem to vary a good deal from one section of the country to another. In Southern California they were a waste of time and I soon gave up on them. Here in Missouri they are a way of life and I picked up quite a considerable number of as-new paperbacks prior to opening my last store. It's a nuisance but you may want to give it a try in your area. Understand, all of these methods are only applicable when it comes to gathering stock before you open your shop. Once you're open for business there'll be no need for any of them; you'll be turning down far more stock than you need. And there's another of the great fears you'll probably have until you've been in the business a while. What if I can't get enough good books? Believe me, it's the least of your worries. What you have to worry about is to avoid the temptation many booksellers succumb to. They can't say no to good stock and they end up with overcrowded shops and renting warehouses where the excess stock sits until it becomes either damaged or so out of vogue as to be worthless. It's a common problem in the industry. Don't let it happen to you.

The solution is quite simple. If that much irresistible material is coming your way it would be foolish to refuse it; but it would be equally foolish to warehouse it. Every dollar you spend on a book should turn over three times per year and become at least three each time but it can scarcely do that if the first book is sitting in storage somewhere. When blessed with a feast of fine books, make room for them! Have a sidewalk sale. Slash prices in the shop. Offer a second book for a dollar. Just *get them in and get them out!* Let me make this just as straightforward as possible. You want to accept every good book on trade or sale offered to you. You want to sell as many books as humanly possible, at least up to the point where you can still replace them. Since replacing stock is the least of your worries you will never have to worry about selling your books too fast. You want the book-buying public in your area to look to you for their needs. That says it all. If in order to do the above you have to discount some of your stock to maintain the balance of incoming books and outgoing books, do it. Don't take the blessing of a heavy influx of nice stock and turn it into a curse by hiding the boxes in your garage until they rot. Too many people in this business have carved their prices and their policies in stone; when you get overloaded, share the wealth with the greatest people in the world — your customers.

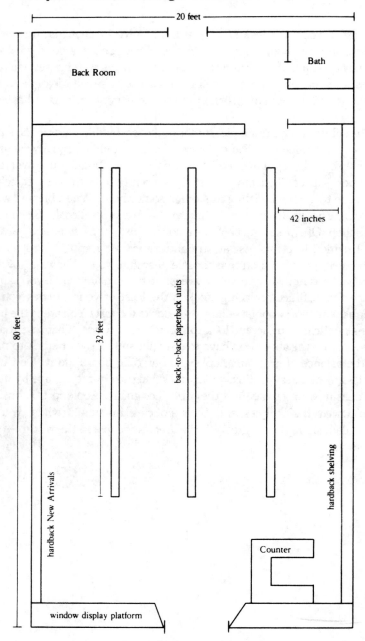

Suggested layout for standard 1600 sq. ft. store

Figure 1

5

Lay It Out and Build It Right— the First Time!

Books are like opportunities, which may be either used, misused, or let alone, with results strictly according to the line of conduct pursued. Books are challenges thrown out by the wisest men to you and me, to think their thoughts, to feel their emotion, and to see with our own eyes their visions of beauty.

J. Rutherford

The following plan has evolved over a period of years through a long process of observation, trial and error. You're well advised to take advantage of my long apprenticeship. The guidelines in this chapter should be applicable regardless of the particular format of the retail space you select.

All outside perimeter walls will accomodate hardback shelving. Paperback shelving will be in the form of back-to-back running rows within the interior of the shop. Figure 1 represents the most common retail space available in a contemporary shopping center. It is, in fact, the precise layout of HOOKED ON BOOKS, the store I built in 1984.

Before we get into the actual construction, now is the time to give some serious consideration to the color and condition of the walls and carpeting. Renewing them before erecting the shelving is a lark; afterward it becomes next to impossible. Suit yourself on the carpet as long as it's a good hotel grade with a short nap, but the walls should definitely be fairly light in color. Sand beige may not strike you as esthetically exciting but it's about as dark as you'd care to go. Eggshell white is better yet.

Next you'll need to think through where some of your subject sections are going to be. This is because there are a few which will require oversized shelving. These sections are Art, Illustrated Books, and Geography. (Atlases are large.) It is a good idea to locate those first two sections near the front of the store where they may be easily monitored from the desk for the simple reason that they will be some of the most expensive books in your store. Geography doesn't matter and all you'll want is one shelf for the atlases. These oversized shelves should measure a good eighteen inches in height to accommodate what is known as a folio-sized book. One anywhere in the store for Geography, two up near the front for Art and two more for Illustrated Books. If you think your personal preference is going to lead you to specialize in either of the two latter subjects then you'd better plan additional folio-sized shelving. (I deliberately omit the possibility of your wanting to specialize in Geography because if you do you'll go bankrupt.) All other hardback shelving will measure as outlined in the coming directions, varying only slightly for attractiveness and ease of construction.

ESTIMATING THE MATERIALS NEEDED

Measure the running length of your total interior wall space, excepting only areas of less than three feet in width such as spaces between doors. Multiply the resulting factor by seven, that being the normal number of shelves you'll be providing all around. Next measure the floor to ceiling height. To ascertain the number of uprights of this size required, divide the running length of your wall space by a factor of six. This seems to be the ideal spacing both to accommodate the length of the material to be found at the lumber stores and to minimize the work of construction without risking sagging shelves after a few years. There's no point in being compulsive about it; each section needn't match in width. When approaching corners or the end of a wall, adjust the width of the last few sections more or less equally so you'll avoid ending up with a final section measuring two or three feet across.

This hardback shelving is to be built of two by eight inch stock. The type of wood will depend on what is reasonable and available in your area. I used something called yellow pine in my last store. It was remarkably inexpensive and entirely suitable. It wasn't finished smoothly and it had knots and even checks in it but that merely serves to give the finished product character. The shelves end up looking as if they've been either distressed or they were taken out of an old barn. The effect is quite charming, so don't feel you have to have satin smooth lumber without a flaw in it.

It isn't necessary to attach this perimeter shelving to the wall. As you'll see later on, it will all tie in with the interior shelving by means of overhead bracing. It makes it slightly more difficult, especially in the beginning, if you are working with a dropped ceiling as opposed to a solid one. This deprives you of the ability to wedge your uprights into place tightly. If this is the case, you will have to at least temporarily fasten your first couple of uprights to the wall.

Next you'll need to estimate the amount of material to order for your paperback shelving. These will be constructed of one by six pine, finished all four sides. They will be constructed in modular units measuring four by eight feet. The backing of each will be a four by eight foot sheet of masonite either one-eighth or three-sixteenths inches thick. The average shop of sixteen hundred square feet as shown in Figure 1 will accommodate fifty-four of these units. Each has a capacity of about one thousand average-sized mass market paperbacks so you can see this allows you to present quite an impressive offering once they're filled.

Each unit requires sixty running feet of one by six inch pine stock and, of course, one sheet of masonite. Measure and sketch out the best layout of your own available retail space and figure out how many of these modular units you'll be able to use. They will run in double back-to-back rows measuring approximately one foot in total width. The beauty of this design is that it gives you an enormous capacity for stock with an absolute minimum loss of floor space. Don't make the all too common mistake of jamming in an extra row of shelving at the cost of ending up with too-narrow aisles. You want your shop to be bright, non-claustraphobic; a place where sensitive people may relax and feel comfortable browsing for long periods of time. It's essential they be able to pass one another easily in the aisles. I've found an aisle width of forty-two inches to be fine. You might shave that figure a couple of inches if your layout demands but certainly no more.

Now you're ready to order the materials. You know the total of two by eights in twelve foot lengths needed. You've multiplied sixty running feet of one by six times the number of paperback units you wish to build. You'll need one sheet of masonite for each unit. Now is the time to take your shopping list around for estimates. This comes to a fair order of lumber and you may be amazed, as I was, at the spread in the quotes you'll be getting. I received estimates fully 35 per cent higher than the price I ultimately paid.

The one by sixes may be ordered in eight foot lengths but it's slightly less expensive to order them in sixteen foot lengths. This may strike you as an awkward size but they are comparatively light and easy to handle; I believe it also saves a bit of time when it comes to finishing them.

TIME TO GET YOUR HANDS DIRTY: PREPPING THE WOOD

Try not to panic when the truck pulls up with all that material. It's going to appear a bit awesome, especially in view of what you're going to have to do with all of it, but hang tough. There's no use denying this is the hardest work you'll ever be faced with in the book business. You're looking at a long tedious job of work and you'd do well to hire a couple of young huskies to help if you can afford the luxury. But please don't cut corners on this part of the program. The result is going to be a shop which bespeaks class for many years to come. It will generate compliments and cash every single day you're in business and you'll be so glad you did it right long after the memory of the drudgery and the aching muscles goes away.

So there it is, that impressively large pile of lumber staring you in the face. First let me give you the good news. You don't have to do any prep work on the masonite sheets so you can forget about that stack for now. Next cover the floor with heavy gauge plastic drop cloths, not the ninety-nine cent flimsies which tear at an angry glance. Overlap them and tape them together in place to make certain the materials you're going to be using won't stain the carpet. Set up a pair of sawhorses for each worker, then put on some work clothes you don't ever want to see again. Rubber gloves help but much more importantly, make absolutely certain you provide the best ventilation possible.

Here it comes! What you're going to have to do is rub stain and sealer over every single bit of all four sides of every one of those darned boards. Whatever you do, make absolutely certain the brand you select is a combination stain AND sealer. Many brands are not both. If you fail to do this you will add a great deal of totally unnecessary work to what is enough of a project already. Use some old towels or similarly rough cloth and just rub the stain and sealer on evenly. It's a simple one-step process and you'll soon get the hang of it. Don't worry about being overly meticulous but at the same time you don't want to leave a lot of swirl marks behind where you applied too much stain. Trust me. It'll look great! Just get it done. As each board is finished there's no other way but to prop it up against the wall to dry, remembering to rub away the hand prints and the bar where it rested upon the sawhorses after placing it against the wall. This is going to leave marks where the boards bear against the wall but that's unavoidable and takes only minutes to touch up later after construction is completed. If the paint job on the walls was good enough that you didn't have to redo them entirely your landlord will have a record of the paint that was used to allow for touch-ups later. On the off chance such information is not in his files, all you have to do is borrow one of those rings of color samples from your nearest full service paint dealer and match it up.

Your choice of finish may be anything that turns you on. I personally dislike the effect of a blond or ash stain. I believe something at least as dark as English walnut is much richer but I freely admit this is a purely subjective opinion.

The raw wood of the two by eights especially will soak up the stain greedily and be ready the following day for the final step in finishing. (The wood will be — you may not.) The next step is to brush on a liberal coating of verathane, polyurethane, or some variation thereof. Just don't use varnish. These newer plastic derivatives will hold up far better. These products come in flat, semi-gloss and high gloss, though they often use euphemisms like satin for flat and bar-top for high gloss. You may think that satin or semi-gloss appears richer than does the bright finish of the high gloss. I agree, but I urge you to use the high gloss. The reason is that high gloss is the toughest finish and flat or satin the poorest. With these products, the less shine the shorter the life expectancy. Besides, within six months it ends up looking like semi-gloss and a year later it's flat.

When you apply the urethane, don't attempt to become an artist and brush it out repeatedly as you might varnish. You should never have to dilute it. This gives it a penchant for running and since you're going to be stacking it at an angle against the wall you could end up with some not-so-nice ripples in the finish. Just brush it on generously with a four inch natural bristle brush and try not to worry too much about it. It flows nicely and there's no reason you shouldn't end up with a professional-looking job. If you glop it on you may get some runs, so it's a good idea to make a check of your first few boards ten or fifteen minutes after you've finished with them and stacked them against the wall. Any runs you find may be brushed out but much longer than that and it's better to leave them because brushing at that point will leave a dull spot and the brush marks will look worse than the run. (Face the fact that you'll have some runs and missed spots but it's not important. You'll take such imperfections into consideration as you build the shelves, hiding the runs on top or bottom shelves where they'll forever remain your secret.) Again, don't forget to brush out your hand prints and the mark where the boards rested upon the sawhorses after placing each board against the wall.

Now, assuming you've survived thus far, there's one more step remaining in the preparation phase. The one by sixes are going to need a second coat of verathane. You'll need about a dozen sheets of one hundred or one hundred and twenty grit sandpaper to rough them up a little in order to get a good bond between the coats. If you skip this little step the second coat will shortly begin sluffing off in large sheets. It doesn't take long, just hit them lightly and don't be afraid of scarring the first coat because it'll all disappear with the final coat. The manufacturer recommends a much finer grit for this kind of work but I've found it goes far faster with a rougher grit and you scarcely have to bear down at all. In fact you mustn't because you could expose the bare wood by removing some of the stain so take it easy. Be certain to dust off the boards well with a tack rag before administering the final coat or you'll end up with a non-skid surface.

You may have noticed I said the one by sixes needed a second coat of urethane but I didn't mention the two by eights. Actually, they need at least one more coat because they soaked up the finish far more than the smoother, smaller shelving, but I've found it's a lot easier to do that after construction is completed. That way all you have to do is the uprights, flat tops of shelves and the leading edges. Since they are somewhat heavier to handle this is quite a savings in time and energy. They too will require a light sanding prior to a second coat.

THE SATISFYING PART: MAKING YOUR SHOP BEAUTIFUL

Seeing the grace and loveliness of your shop coming to life around you more than makes up for all the drudgery you've just gone through. You'll need to assemble the following tools: seven inch circular saw, hand saw, electric drill, level, square (make certain it's square; they aren't always.), hammer, nail punch and tape measure.

Measure carefully from floor to ceiling at the most logical place for your exterior hardback shelving to begin. Always check the butt end you are NOT going to cut with the square. You must never assume any board was delivered to you with squared ends. When making the cut for the bottom of each upright, give it just the slightest angle. Nothing more than a degree or two so that the heel will be slightly shorter than the outward toe. This serves to force the weight of the upright, and the attendant shelving, back against the wall. If you are working with a suspended drop ceiling you'll be unable to wedge the upright tightly into position as you would normally do if you had a solid ceiling. In this case it will be necessary to utilize crossing nails, one driven at an angle from each side of the upright high up near the ceiling in order to secure that first upright in position. If good fortune provides a stud inside the wall where these nails enter they should be driven home with a nail punch and left permanent. Most likely they will not and should be only temporary, only driven in far enough to secure the upright until it becomes a part of the first completed unit. Use your level to insure that it is perpendicular.

Select a full length twelve foot board with squared butts and place it on the floor tightly against your first upright. At the opposite end of this floor board, measure and set in your second upright, securing it as you did the first. I'm assuming you're working with something akin to the standard eight foot ceiling. If not, this next measurement won't hold true but nothing else changes. Measure about thirteen inches down from the ceiling and make a straight line at ninety degrees to your uprights. Use your square. These lines obviously represent a level shelf. On these lines drive in two four inch galvanized nails at a forty-five degree angle from below. They should penetrate at least an inch into the uprights. These nails now form the rest on which you are going to place that board on the floor until it can be permanently secured. I specify galvanized nails because their roughness gives them a holding power nearly equal to that of a screw. Once the shelf board is in place, resting upon those slanted nails, drill three pilot holes through the uprights into the butt of the shelf. Use a small enough bit so that when the nails are driven home they will bite hard. Do not drill very far into the butt to further insure a tight hold. When the nails are flush with the wood, countersink them slightly with your nail punch. For this initial section it will be necessary to have someone brace a board against the opposite side as you're driving in the nails. After this first section is completed you'll find you can easily work solo if necessary.

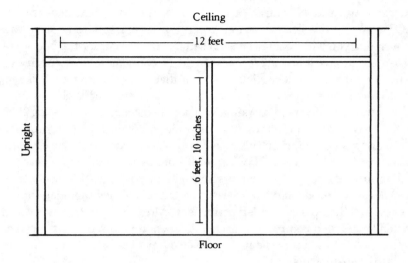

Figure 2

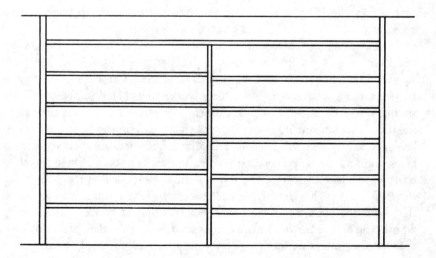

Completed hardback unit

Figure 3

Now you may remove those four angled nails which held up the initial shelf. This is the procedure you will use to position each shelf in preparation for securing it permanently. Get used to constantly checking with your level before nailing each shelf in place.

Find and mark the exact center of the shelf you've just secured. Measure from the bottom of the shelf at that center point to the floor. It should come out somewhere around six feet eleven inches, again assuming an eight foot ceiling. Cut a board to fit. It should wedge into position snugly but not so that it causes the top shelf to bow upward. Don't forget to cut a little extra off the heel of the upright so that it tends to bear against the wall. Check to see that it's perpendicular, then drive home three nails from the top of the shelf down into the top of this center upright. You now have the nucleus of your first shelving unit as shown in Figure 2.

Next you're going to build in another six shelves from that top one down to the bottom, the lowest one of which will rest on the floor. The thickness of these boards is actually one and three-quarters or perhaps only one and five-eighths inches. Deduct the total width of those six shelves and you end up with approximately seventy-four inches. Divide this available space up into six shelf heights somewhat at random. The minimum height should be ten and one-half inches. This is adequate to accommodate an average 8 vo hardback book. The idea is not to make every shelf the exact same height as all the others. It looks far better to vary them a little and each subsequent section will have to have staggered shelving anyway in order to be able to nail into the next row of shelving. So make some as small as ten and one-half inches and others as much as twelve inches in height. After completing the first half, do the same on the second half and you'll end up with a completed section as shown in Figure 3.

There you have the basic hardback shelving unit. All you have to do is duplicate that unit all around the perimeter of the store. Remember to stagger the top twelve-foot shelf just as you have the others so you can get at the butts to nail it into place. Vary the placement of that top shelf up and down as you go so you don't end up with a top shelf too near the ceiling to accommodate any books.

All should go well until you reach your first inside corner. Outside corners are no problem because you end up with two uprights at right angles to one another, but inside corners call for a hollow box upright as shown in Figure 4. This is merely two uprights, measured carefully for proper length. Lap one edge over the other, it doesn't matter which, then drive

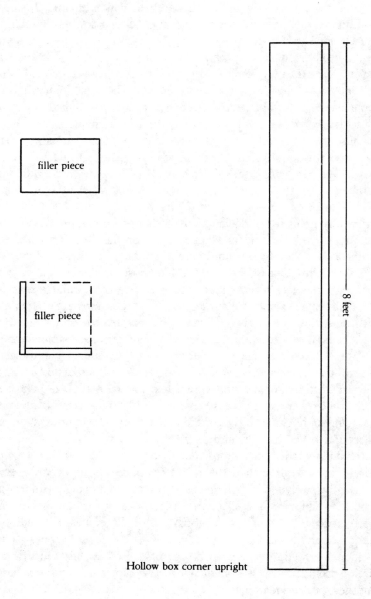

filler piece

filler piece

Hollow box corner upright

8 feet

Figure 4

home a nail about every eighteen inches through the overlap into the leading edge of the second board. Then it'll be necessary to cut three filler pieces which will bear against the wall when the two uprights are snugged into place. The reason for this is that you'll be forced to toenail these shelves from beneath into these uprights and if not for the fillers they wouldn't maintain their positions but would merely be driven into the corner away from the oncoming nails. Place one filler high, one low and one near the center. Toenailing that second shelf from the bottom is a little tricky but it can be done. All the bottom shelves which rest on the floor may merely be wedged into place and no fastenings are necessary. The corner uprights, once they are in place, give the appearance of a massive solid beam and are very attractive.

CONSTRUCTION TECHNIQUES FOR PAPERBACK SHELVING UNITS

Since these modular units are each identical you can get a little assembly line going, cutting all of your boards to size at once. It would be wise to assemble a test unit first just to make sure you've grasped the principle though. Each unit consists of two eight-foot lengths of one by six — these are the sides — and eleven shelves measuring forty-six and one-half inches. That is, four feet minus the inch and a half width of the two side uprights. The bottom shelf will be flush with the floor and each shelf will be exactly seven and three-quarters inches in height. A mass-market sized paperback is seven inches high so this gives you maximum capacity with ease of getting them on and off the shelf. Mass-market refers to the normal sized book we think of as a "pocketbook." The larger paperbacks which are now becoming more popular in lieu of hardbacks are known as trade-sized paperback. These will be filed with the hardbacks, since it would be terribly wasteful to build your paperback shelves high enough to handle the relatively few you'll have in stock.

You'll soon get so you can knock out one of these units in about twenty minutes after you've done a few. Start by carefully marking one eight foot long upright to be used as a template for all the others. Beginning at the bottom, draw a line parallel with the butt and three-quarters of an inch wide. This represents the actual thickness of the one by six shelving and designates the location of the bottom shelf. Then carefully measure seven

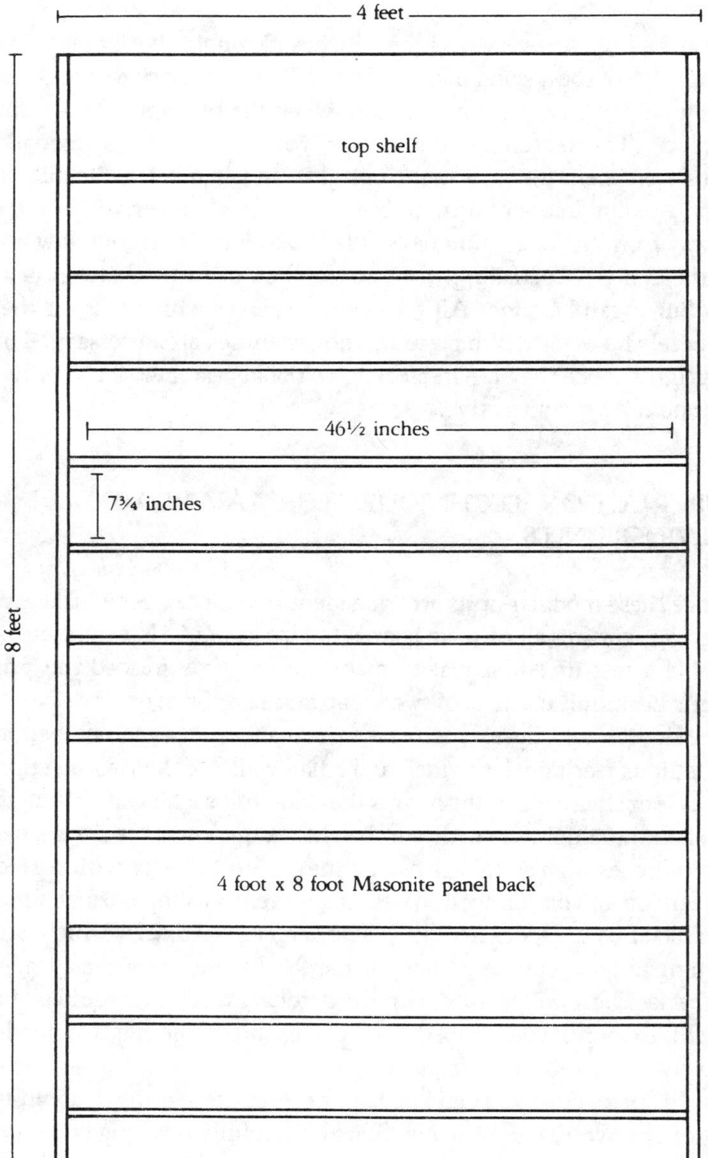

Modular paperback shelving unit

Figure 5

and three-quarters of an inch above the first line and draw another line at exactly ninety degrees to the upright using your square. This is followed by another line three-quarters of an inch above. This marks the location of the second shelf from the bottom. Continue this process until you have eleven double lines, each three-quarters of an inch apart, each pair of lines exactly seven and three-quarters inches from the others. The top shelf will come out somewhat over that and be open at the top. In other words, there will be no shelf attached to the top of the uprights.

As soon as you've completed marking one upright in this manner it becomes a simple matter to lay it alongside each of the others, making certain the butts are flush, then using your square to extend these marks over onto the other. If your square is long enough you may even lay an upright on either side of your master template and knock them off two at a time.

Lay one of the sheets of masonite down on the floor to gain a smooth working surface, then stand two of your marked uprights on edge, parallel, flush with the edges of the masonite panel. Take your pre-cut forty-six and a half inch shelving, position them against the uprights on their marks and nail them in place. For this purpose use a two inch galvanized box nail, taking care not to miss the meat of the shelving and come out above or below it. If you're the fussy type, care may be given to matching the grain and finish used in each unit for there will be some variation. Once all eleven shelves are fastened to both uprights, lay a sheet of masonite over the top and fasten it with the same nails, one every couple of feet. Don't worry if there is a slight variation in the thickness of some of the boards and they aren't all absolutely flush at the back. One of the reasons you built the unit face-down on a hard surface was to insure they would all be flush at the front where it shows. Always begin fastening the panel at one of the bottom corners, making certain the edge of the masonite is flush with the outside of the wood all the way around. And that's all there is to that. See Figure 5.

It might be a good idea to have someone assist you in drawing a line across the back of the masonite panel by lining up the shelving nails on each side. This line would correspond to the location of each shelf and it would be a good idea to put a few nails toward the center of each shelf from the back to prevent any possibility of future sag. I've not done this but I wish I had and of course it would be an unthinkable job to do it now. It doesn't seem to be a major problem since the panel itself tends to force the unit to hold its shape and a four foot shelf of paperbacks isn't all that much of a load anyway. But a slight bow has occurred in some of my shelves after a few years and it's so simple to do at the time of construction I believe you'd be well advised to do it.

After you've completed construction of the appropriate number of these units it will be time to jockey them into position. They may be moved easily enough by placing something like a piece of heavy paper under them and pulling them like a sled. They are heavy and not at all stable standing alone so be careful. In fact, as you complete each one, you should lean them against a wall rather than trusting them to stand upright.

Set the first two in place, back-to-back, then use a six inch length of one by two or any suitable piece from your scrap pile to tie them together at the top. This piece should span the tops of one side of the first two uprights and be nailed down to them so that they become one solid unit. As the next pair go into position beside them the top brace will then fasten into four uprights instead of two — the distal pair of the first set of opposing shelving and the touching pair of the second back-to-back set. As you build your row, remember to keep measuring from the base of the hardback shelving parallel opposite to make certain your row is straight and your aisle width is consistent. Also make sure all the units are tight up against one another at the base. An inch and a half nail through the upright of each succeeding shelving unit into the one before will serve to bind them together nicely until you can add the bracing at the top. While the units are not very stable alone, they tend to become quite stable when fastened back-to-back and side-by-side in rows. In the end when you brace them into the hardback shelving around the perimeter of the store they are very stable indeed.

When all your paperback units are in position and fastened together, you'll need about sixteen lengths of one by two inch stock. Length should be ten or twelve feet feet each. These will make up the braces which will finally serve to tie all the shelving in the shop firmly into place. Use four of these braces to tie your middle banks of paperback shelving together by simply nailing them in place across the aisles with one end fixed to each of the opposing banks. Install one about every eight feet. They first need to be stained to match and they make convenient places to hang signs outlining the subject sections to be found within those aisles. When all your middle shelving is thus firmly braced together overhead, run similar bracing from the hardback shelving along the walls over to the nearest interior bank of paperback shelving. After that it will be all strongly fixed in place and the beauty of it is the more books you shelve the more secure it becomes.

Don't forget to put that second coat of urethane on the hardback shelving, omitting the undersides. You'll still have to rough up the surface of the first coat in order to achieve good bonding. If you've elected to use rough-finished lumber as I have, a third coat is really in order. At the very least, apply a third coat to the leading edges and the top flat surfaces where the books will rest. A rustic, distressed finish is desirable but you don't want such a rough surface on the top of the shelves that it will tend to abrade your books as they are taken on and off the shelves.

BUILDING THE MONEY BIN: OTHERWISE KNOWN AS THE CHECKOUT COUNTER

This is really all that remains of the construction phase. The counter should always be located in the front of the store, just to one side or other of the door. The size and shape will be dictated by the constraints of your shop. Ideally it should be a rectangle, open at the back, measuring somewhere around five feet on the parallel sides and six feet across the front. Forty-six inches has evolved as the ideal height. The counter top should be sixteen inches in width all around. None of these particular measurements are carved in stone but they have worked well for me in the past.

Simply frame it in with two by fours and then sheath the outside with three-eighths inch plywood with an A side so that it can be stained and finished to match the shelving. Use half-inch plywood for the counter top, cutting it flush with the sides; then nail a lip of one by two inch stock all around the outside and flush with the top. This serves to give you a fine little overhang which looks great after you've covered the top of the counter and this lip with formica. Since this top will be entirely covered with formica there's no point in buying A finish which is considerably more expensive. C grade both sides will serve as well.

If you've never used formica it's not all that tricky as long as you're working in about seventy degree temperatures or more. Just bear in mind that once you touch the glued formica to the glued plywood — that's it! There's no such thing as jockeying it around afterwards so it's a job for two and slow and easy is the watchword. First cut the formica for the outside of the lip and cut it to fit. Leave about an eighth of an inch excess when you cut the pieces for the top. Once it's well set, sand off the excess carefully using a sanding block and eighty grit sandpaper. There's no reason you shouldn't end up with a lovely, professional-looking job.

The final step is the greatest favor you can ever do for your back and shoulder muscles. Lay a bed of the leftover one by sixes you'll undoubtedly have from your paperback shelving units all around the inside base of your counter. Then add cross-bracing from side to side about a foot and a half apart. The one by sixes are standing on edge, you understand, thus creating a platform nearly six inches higher than the surrounding floor. Over this bed you will want to lay a flooring of plywood, in two fitted pieces so that you are able to get it into position. Nail this well into place, particularly around the edges. This will give you an considerable height advantage which will greatly fascilitate the handling of all those wonderful books you're going to be accepting and dispensing over that counter.

Next you will stain the outside of the counter using the same stain as you've selected for the shelving. Add at least two and preferably three coats of urethane. The wide grain of A-sided fir plywood should be most attractive when finished.

You'll find it convenient to position a small desk under one side of the counter top inside this checkout stand. This provides a platform for your cash register which isn't readily accessible to anyone on the other side of the counter. It also provides some much-needed drawer space. That's it for the sweat and blister part of the antiquarian book business. You will want to throw together some sort of work and research table in the back room. It's also a terrific boon to have some shelving back there; you'll probably have enough scraps of lumber left over. It's a good place to use all those boards with the holidays on them, the runs and swirls and fingerprints and spots which were missed entirely. At least I assume you'll have such boards; I know I always did.

6
Getting Ready for the Grand Opening

A book is important when it illuminates the long struggle of men to understand themselves and their world, to be free, and to establish the spirit of wisdom, truth, justice, toleran-ce, kindness, and beauty. The age of the book does not mat-ter. It may have been published five years ago, a century ago, five centuries ago, and if it fulfills these criteria it is important.

Stanley Pergellis

PROVEN SUBJECT SECTIONS WHICH SHOULD BE STOCKED

For those of you whose dream of the ideal antiquarian book shop features row upon row of burnished leather bindings and bright dust jackets it's time for some harsh reality. It's the day of the paperback. The current generation no longer considers the paperback as just a cheap throw-away, something you stick in your pocket and take to the beach. They were brought up on paperbacks; their textbooks in school were paperbacks. They no longer hold them in contempt as my generation once did. (And at upwards of four dollars for a mass market-sized novel they're scarcely "cheap.")

An enterprising dealer ran an ad in the BOOKS FOR SALE section of the AB a couple of years ago featuring all paperbacks. Later he wrote an editorial telling of the success of the ad and the prices realized from his offering and chiding his peers for failing to recognize that there are collec-table paperbacks and that the old attitudes toward pocket books won't wash anymore. He's right! After you've seen copies of Burroughs' *Naked Lunch* sell for over a hundred dollars you begin to get the idea.

Chapter 8 will deal with the collectable aspects of paperback and hard-back books. Right now we need to consider the kinds of books you'll want to concentrate on as you build your stock.

Now try not to gag but in all probability the most active paperback section — and that means THE most active section — is going to be Harlequin Romances. They are far and away the most widely-read of any of the genre fiction being published today. There are any number of reasons why this is so. Creative, aggressive marketing is one; readers receive them direct from the publisher by joining "clubs," perhaps receiving an average of one a week. Many belong to a number of clubs. Another theory, which seems reasonable, is they allow women to fantasize about some of the old traditional values which are in short supply in these days of liberated thinking. Apparently the idea of the dominant male and the submissive female and gallantry and romance as opposed to meaningless sex still has enormous appeal, if only as a fantasy.

This will certainly be one of your largest sections so set aside half a dozen of the paperback shelving units just for Harlequins. There are at least a couple of dozen different "runs" or "clubs," with new ones coming out fast. They look remarkably alike except for color and publisher's logo. Unlike the other sections in the store, these books will be shelved by number, not in alphabetical order by the author. This is the way their readers keep track of what they've read; many carry little notebooks recording the numbers they already have. (The publishers claim plenty of men read them, too, but I've yet to see it.)

So shelve these in numerical sequence, keeping each club separate. There is something you must avoid when it comes to Harlequins and that is taking in any of the older ones. This entire genre has changed so markedly in the past four or five years that the older ones are virtually unsaleable. The new ones are much "spicier" (some critics even refer to them as porn.) This development has blown the older type completely out of the water. Of course there is also the fact that most everybody who might have wanted to read them has already done so. You can easily tell the difference just by the cover price. Anything under $1.75 original publisher's price is surely too dated to deserve shelf space. You'll soon get to recognize the undesirable ones, such as CANDLELIGHT REGENCY and a host of others. The world is chock full of them and you'll be offered tons. You must avoid them like the plague. Locate the Harlequins somewhere near the back of the shop because these clients require no assistance and they tend to block the aisles with their great stacks of books. They often read a couple a day — God bless 'em — and are prodigious buyers of books.

General Fiction will be the largest paperback section in the store. It warrants eight or nine units of shelving. It must be alphabetically arranged if you ever hope to do a volume business. It's an eye-crossing chore to set it up that first time but easy to maintain and it's one of the biggest keystones to your success. It's one of those non-negotiable rules I mentioned earlier. Most of the unsuccessful stores don't do it. I had a so-called bookseller once tell me he didn't do it because it forced his customers to scan through all of his titles instead of just checking to to see if the few books they wanted were there. Thus, his theory went, they were certain to come across other provocative titles and end up buying more books. I was sorely tempted to ask him what his theory was which prevented keeping the store clean. Such rationalizations are nothing other than an excuse for laziness. What it actually does is force the buyer to throw up his hands in disgust and leave — for good. It is nothing less than an insult to your customers to expect them to scan thousands of titles and authors in hope of finding what they want.

Nearly as large will be your Historical Romance section. This genre has become amazingly popular and some of our best writers are now working within it. It's easy to recognize these books. They are almost always thick, featuring a man and a woman in period costume on the cover. In fact the covers almost all look exactly alike, invariably showing a rather ripe girl with lots of decolletage in a man's arms. Many of these books are part of ongoing series. They sell exceedingly well and you will want to set aside half-a-dozen units exclusively for them. You must never mix these in with general fiction — a mistake most stores make — because those who read historicals usually want nothing else and the easier you make it for them the more they'll buy and the more faithful they'll be for the simple fact you're fulfilling their needs. Most of these books are fairly well researched and often well-written. You can pick up a lot of history in a painless manner reading them. If there was ever an example of not being able to judge a book by its cover this is it.

Next in importance, or at least in size, will probably be Science Fiction & Fantasy. This may vary with geographical location somewhat but I doubt there's anywhere in the country this section would not be one of your mainstays. This genre has never been healthier and is even gaining respectability with the critics. Some wonderful writing is being done in this area.

Its devotees can devour books almost on a scale with the Harlequin readers. Allocate another half-dozen units of paperback shelving to this subject section. Some stores segregate Fantasy from Science Fiction. Don't do it! It's extremely confusing; for one thing a high percentage of the writers have done both. Then you're faced with the ridiculous question of whether to put each author in one or the other section or divide his titles. Neither is satisfactory. Order is one thing; compulsiveness is another.

Space will be devoted to the question of values of paperback Science Fiction in Chapter 8. Unlike Harlequins, the older the Science Fiction book and the lower the cover price the better. This will be the single most difficult section to fill because Fantasy readers tend to be collectors. They hold onto their books. You will find, however, once you establish a section it will sustain itself. This will be one of the very few sections where some paperbacks will be worth far more than half the cover price. If the collector activity in your area warrants, you may well want to package first paperback printings of important titles in plastic bags. This appraises the noncollector that they are special and it also protects them, since condition is vital when it comes to collectable paperbacks. The price may be written on the plastic bag with a marker.

Your next section in both size and dollar volume will undoubtedly be Mystery/Adventure. It's another very healthy area of publishing right now. It's also unique, as is Science Fiction, in that there is equal interest in both hot new titles and the old classics. It is just as difficult to keep old Christie and Stout titles on the shelf as it is the latest Ludlum. This makes it nice for you because it's easier to get to know what to accept for stock — almost anything!

Here again you have a loyal cadre of aficionados who usually buy little else but they gobble up ''Whodunnits'' like popcorn. I confess to being a member in good standing of this club. As with Science Fiction, the older volumes with low cover prices are not a problem here. Quite the contrary. Many of the old Dell and Ace twenty-five cent and thirty-five cent pocket books are true collectors' items and may be worth surprising amounts. More concerning that in Chapter 8. Nothing much to be aware of here other than the usual no-no's such as worn and shabby books and titles you already have six copies of.

Next in order of importance should be Westerns. This section is a steady producer and warrants at least two units of shelving. Take whatever you can get in saleable condition regardless of cover price. The only unusual thing about this section is a single author — Louis L'Amour. You can't just file Louis in with all the other Western writers because clients will bring in common writers for trade and take all your Louis and you'll never have any on the shelf. His popularity is unprecedented among contemporary Western writers; many people read him who wouldn't be caught dead reading any other Westerns. He's the only Western writer I can think of who's currently being published in hardback.

What you have to do is set Louis up with his own little section next to the other Westerns but with the shelf clearly labelled CASH ONLY. You will, of course, allow trades for other L'Amours. The other thing you need to do is impose a one dollar minimum on his paperbacks, clearly stating this on the shelf as well. People have never objected to this in my stores. There are a lot of old L'Amours out there with seventy-five cent cover prices. The dollar minimum enables you to pay enough to continue receiving these desirable books.

A word concerning condition of Western paperbacks. For some reason which has always eluded me, you cannot apply the same standards of condition to Westerns as you may to every other subject. If you did you'd never have nearly enough, and the clients who buy them don't seem to mind when they're a bit dog-eared. Perhaps it's the type of steely-eyed man of action who reads these books; most of them come in looking as if they have been through a range war. For a long time I rejected them as I would any others but I got tired of never having many and lowered my standards and it's worked out fine.

Next in line will be Horror Fantasy. This was a very minor section when I first started learning the antiquarian book business but, due almost entirely to the brilliant career of a young man named Stephen King, the subject is expanding very quickly. This is going to be one of your most active sections. Two units should be enough for now because there haven't been enough books published to sate the public's appetite but this section will continue to grow.

Theater is next; this includes all books about movies or theater, biographies, technical books on directing or filmmaking, everything pertaining to the entertainment industry. (Including Television.) It will consist mostly of star biographies and will do moderately well. It will never require more than half a unit of shelving at most.

Plays should be adjacent to Theater but a separate section. All books published in a play format should go here.

Classics is a fine section; always very active. It deserves two units of shelving. There isn't much to worry about as far as taking in junk because junk doesn't last long enough to become "classic." There is a good deal of subjectivity involved in determining just what does and does not go into this section. Of course Dickens, Twain and Tolstoy go, but what about Mailer, Kozinski? The answer should be, put them where you think they'll sell best.

History will always pay its way but it's too easy to fill up too large a space with six-month-wonders which nobody wants to buy anymore. Give it half a unit but beware of accepting titles like *Report of the Warren Commission* or *The White House Transcripts* which pretty much everybody who would ever want to has already read. Very contemporary material is good and so is material about fifteen or twenty years older or more but there's that area in between where there doesn't seem to be much interest.

Philosophy is as good or better than History. Take pretty much whatever you can get; you'll never be overloaded here. I believe it's a good idea to keep Eastern Philosophy separate. Both sections shouldn't require more than half a unit of shelving.

Psychology is OK; worth about a third of a unit. Older classics still do well here. Titles such as *I'm OK; You're OK,* so not much to worry about here.

Health and Diet is tricky. Give it a third of a unit but be aware that diet and health books are very faddish. They may make a big splash upon publication but good luck on selling most of them a couple of years down the road. Of course, good solid medical references like *Gray's Anatomy* or *Merck Manual* are solid sellers but you can't give away an old diet book. That includes even the biggest of the best-selling ones. Exercise books do well.

Metaphysics is quite an active section, in spite of the fact that even those who read a great deal of it tell me the vast majority of it is nonsense of the first water. The main thing you want to avoid here is any book dealing with UFO's (No interest there anymore). Hottest fads right now seem to be pyramid power and reincarnation. (It's OK; you don't have to read it — just sell it!.)

I always maintain an ethnic section. Here, of course, is where you'll see the greatest variation regionally. If you set up shop near the Mexican border you're going to do a brisk business in Hispanic Culture.

In New York City I'd imagine you'd want to devote a good deal of space to Jewish Culture. This one you'll have to play by ear but the section is bound to be worthwhile wherever you set up shop.

Religion has never been very productive, other than good references and unusual books. There is such a sea of wimpy books, half of which were never even sold in stores but sent out as premiums from repentance mongers with a radio or TV show, that it's easy to fill up shelves with them but to no avail. Obviously you'll want a Religion section but there are very few paperbacks you'll want in it. Delegate a shelf or two and be careful how you fill it because these books aren't "keepers" and your customers will be trying to palm them off on you constantly.

A small paperback section is called for to contain everything conected with maternity, marriage, babies, babies names and family. I've never been sure what to call it; maybe you can come up with something better than Mother & Child. It's worth a couple of shelves.

War is a brisk-selling section. It requires two units of shelving and must be divided up into War: Fiction and War: Non-Fiction. Here again, age is no problem; the older the better. As long as you avoid getting sixteen copies of *Thirty Seconds Over Tokyo* you'll be fine.

Business and Self-Help is a fairly good section as long as you don't clutter it up with ten-year-old books on the stock market and real estate. These books must be contemporary, with the obvious classic exceptions such as the books of Carnegie, Peale and a few others. Self-help books move especially well; books on improving your memory, becoming a better salesman, books for women in the business world, all are in demand.

Sexual studies is a valid, though not particularly lucrative, section. I've always had a shelf of references but I must admit I wouldn't have hurt myself much if I hadn't. Your option.

Contemporary Women's is a section my wife dreamed up about eight years ago. It was one of her better ideas. There is a surprising amount of literature available which fits into this section — everything from *The Cracker Factory* to *The Women's Room.* It warrants several shelves and it's entirely possible it may take more in the future.

Reference is composed of just that: dictionaries, thesauruses, books of quotations, encyclopedias, almanacs, et cetera. It's a good solid section and worth all the room you can fill. The trouble is these are the last books anyone usually wants to get rid of. Things to avoid are fairly obvious: old sets of encyclopedias, broken sets (missing volumes), outdated anything unless it's classic material (you cannot sell a 1975 almanac). I've had little luck selling any encyclopedias other than Britannica III. Ever since they came out with their new format in 1972 — Macropedia and Micropedia — that's the one everybody seems to want. Oh, I've sold an occasional set of World Book and Americana and I wouldn't turn down a recent set if I didn't already have one on the shelf but Britannica is the one you can sell most easily. This also goes for Britannica's fifty-four volume set of Great Books. This set sells well, especially in the moroccan binding.

Americana is one of your best subject sections but not too much of it is going to be in paperback format. In fact, so little of it is that I don't maintain a paperback section at all but file the wrapped items in with the hardbacks. (Wrapped refers to a paperbound book.)

How-To is a kind of a catch-all section containing everything from auto repair, home repair and crafts to gardening and collectors' references. It's a bit of a mare's nest but it would be worse if you divided them all up into another fifteen or twenty sections. It's a fun, active section where you'll always wish you had more material.

Biographies is a section containing all such life histories other than the film and theater people. American presidents and historical characters from the middle ages seem to be most popular. Give it no more than half a unit of shelving.

True Crime requires two or three shelves. There is an active interest in reading books about contemporary mass murderers, as well as classic criminals. Worth stocking but one of the poorer sections.

Large Print Books is just that. You'll notice certain publishers over the years have put out books with oversized print, mostly for the convenience of elderly readers or those with eye problems. You will earn the everlasting gratitude of your clients if you file these books in a section of their own. Give it half a unit of shelving and put everything in there in large print format, whether it be history, western or romance.

Sports will require two or three shelves. The hottest subjects seem to be body-building and martial arts, but baseball, basketball and football all do well just as the seasons begin. Golf is a perennial best seller, too.

Games will be a very small section but worth having. Chess and checkers have always been the steady movers but now there is an increasing amount of material on puzzles and brain-games and the kids seem to love them. Rulebooks and how-to books on gambling and card games are steady sellers as well.

Humor is a very good section and deserves half a unit. Here you'll file all the cartoon books such as *Peanuts*, as well as the humorous paperbacks by best-sellers like Bombeck and Buchwald. Minimal concern here about what material to take; older material does well, too.

Natural history deserves several shelves. There will always be an interest in bird and animal books. Beware of accumulating too many of some which have enjoyed enormous sales, however, such as the James Herriot books.

Science rates about the same as Natural History — maybe three shelves. There's not much point in stocking outdated material unless it's a hundred years old or more. After that it becomes of interest again. Math and astronomy seem to do the best, along with well-written general interest books such as Carl Sagan's *Cosmos* and Asimov's *Intelligent Man's Guide to Science.*

There remain a handful of sections of minor consequence, such as Drugs, Music & Dance, and Travel. Devote no more than a shelf apiece to them.

SHELVING OF HARDBACK BOOKS

It is my custom to locate hardback subject sections as nearly opposite their paperback sections as possible. You can do this if you place all the paperback fiction on shelving within the center of the shop, leaving all outside paperback shelving available for nonfiction. Then set up your hardback sections of the same subject right across the aisle from the paperbacks. I've tried commingling paper and hard bound books on the same shelving in the past and found it to be a terrible waste of available space. This system seems to work best. Of course, none of your fiction sections will be adjacent to one another but that seems to be the lesser of the optional evils.

Everything we've just stated concerning paperback sections applies equally as well to hardbacks. The relative amount of space to be alloted to hardbacks will correspond to what I've outlined for paperbacks. Some of your sections will ebb and flow with the arrival and the depletion of suitable material so you will find yourself shifting books from time to time.

There are a few subject sections we still need to discus; these are the ones where no paperback section was suggested. Art is one of these. Most of your art books will be hardback and many of the paper bound ones will be oversized so all art books may be mixed together in one section. If you followed my suggestion in Chapter 5 and built a couple of oversized shelves near the front of the store specifically for art, that's where it all goes. In this section, there is no real reason to have the books in any particular order.

Engineering and Architecture will be a small but worthwhile section without a corresponding paperback section.

Geography should have an oversized shelf earmarked for it somewhere and there will be no paperback section.

Foreign Languages is a valuable perennial, though which languages enjoy popularity will vary with your region of the country. In Southern California, Spanish was the big mover. In the Ozarks I couldn't give away a book on Spanish but German seemed popular. The classic languages always do well, especially Latin. Dictionaries are the most in demand and should be filed here rather than in Reference with English dictionaries.

Anthropology deserves a shelf somewhere; a bottom one will do. It's a fact that books shelved on the topmost and bottom shelves are slow to sell. Simple logic — they don't get the exposure.

Hunting and Fishing is one of your better sections, at least it has been always for me. Again, paper bound books tend to be trade-sized anyway so you'll just need one section.

Illustrated Books should also be near the front of the store with a couple of folio-sized shelves specially built for it. There are few illustrated books of any merit which are paperbound — Maxfield Parrish's Poster Book comes to mind as an exception — so no wraps section is needed.

Children's Books also tend to be oversized and oddly-shaped so it's advisable to commingle all the children's literature in one hardback section. Don't bother trying to keep this section in any kind of order for obvious reasons. It's the only section in the store where the little people will be allowed to handle the books.

Then there's the Old Children's Books; the little people are certainly not encouraged to handle the books in this section because they are very old and fragile and quite lovely. Naturally there is no similar paperback section. This is a good section if you can fill it with suitable stock. All the old nursery rhyme books, children's series such as the Rover Boys, old Scouting books, all are ardently sought by collectors or just clients who remember having them as children. Any of these books which feature nice color plates will go in Illustrated Books.

The last but certainly not the least of the hardback sections is the first one a customer sees when he walks in the door. It is called New Arrivals.

This is where you will shelve new books as they come in for sale or trade each day. They will remain there until slow time in the shop allows you to distribute them into their appropriate sections. The beauty of this system is that your regulars love to pop in and survey New Arrivals; it gives them the opportunity to see what's come in that day without checking all of their pet sections. It becomes quite a treat for them and many a book shelved on New Arrivals will never last long enough to see its section.

When setting up your hardback novel section, segregate old novels, say anything pre-1920. This is always a good idea when you're catering to two entirely different sets of clients. Don't allot much space to the old ones but some of the books are so beautifully bound they do rate a few shelves. The contemporary novel section should be just that; anything much over ten years old should either be in the Classic section or forget it. Hardback novels do not sell at all well for reasons which escape me. People will pay more for a paperback of the same title. It must be either they're so conditioned to think of hardbacks as expensive they don't even consider them or perhaps all their shelving at home is sized to accept only paperbacks.

SHELVING YOUR BOOKS SO THEY SELL

Paperback shelving is designed so that the books may be most attractively displayed by placing them all the way back against the masonite panel. This presents a flush, uniform appearance which is appealing to the eye and simple to maintain. Once in a while it is only necessary to walk up and down the aisles with any old straight edge such as a folio-sized book and even up the books by shoving them all the way back on the shelf. It may sound like a small detail but your degree of success will be determined by such small details. The first impression projected by your shop is all-important.

Hardbacks are not uniform in size, so they must be arranged differently. If you develop the habit of staightening your books whenever you are walking down an aisle it will be quite easy to maintain your hardbacks flush with the front of their shelving. Your customers will soon realize and appreciate what you are attempting to do and they will do their part. It is up to you to establish the pattern of your shop; if you keep a sloppy store your customers will act accordingly.

You can learn a lot about creative display of books with a visit to your local new book store. They make the most of comparatively few books; so would you if you had their cost of inventory. If there's slop on your paperback shelving, a few select books displayed face out serve to take up the slack and increases sales. Cover art on paperbacks sells books, just as creative dust wrappers on hardback books do.

When space permits on New Arrivals, you can make an attractive display of some of your more colorful hardbacks by turning them face out. Creative window displays are a must. The books used for display must be changed at least a couple of times a month for several reasons. One is that you never want to give the impression your stock is going stale; another is the fact that the sun can bleach out the colors on a dust jacket in a remarkably short time.

Interesting things may be done with those lucite cubes when it comes to displays in the windows. If you can't come up with some of those, plywood cubes painted brightly are useful, though the transparency of the lucite is better. Never interfere too much with people's ability to see in and out of your windows clearly.

There is another product available which is helpful in selling your better view or illustrated books. It is known as a Torah stand. They are available in both wood and lucite. They are low book stands designed to hold an OPEN book, thus displaying an appealing color plate, photograph, map or what have you. The wooden ones are to be found at flea markets and antique shops; the lucite ones are available from BRODART, INC. (See Chapter 19.)

It remains for you to conceive of some method to display your expensive collectable books. You can't just file them on open shelves because that causes problems. Non-collectors will get their hands on them and—not appreciating them for what they are—assume your prices are insane and leave. Some of the books will be quite old and should not be handled except by collectors who presumably know what they're doing. My personal preference is to have a few lawyer's bookcases in the front of the store. These are the handsome wood cases with glass hatches in front which lift out and up, then slide back into the case above the books. These are readily available anywhere and modern replicas are as serviceable as genuine antiques. There should also be shelving behind your desk or checkout counter where valuable books may be displayed.

SUPPLIES AND EQUIPMENT

The list is blessedly brief but there are a few things you'll want to pick up prior to Opening Day.

You'll need a step-stool for each aisle in the store. They are helpful for clients to sit on while searching your lower shelves and absolutely necessary for them to stand on to gain access to the top shelving. These are available in many department stores, via their catalogue if not in stock. The ones I use are just plastic and cost about seven or eight dollars each. The metal ones with castors cost four or five times that and don't serve any better. The plastic ones I've used can be purchased at Sears; they are heavy-duty, with the color baked in and I like them better than the expensive metal ones from Brodart. The metal ones have rubber treads which eventually come loose and they have wheels which can be dangerous at times.

You'll also want to obtain a three-step kitchen ladder to enable clients of average height or below to work your topmost shelves in comfort and safety. This is where you put your literary sets and encyclopedias; these books tend to be heavy so you need good access. These short ladders also feature a hand rail and are available at most hardware or department stores.

We've already established the fact that you need a cash register and a desk calculator. If you can find an old hand crank cash register it's just the thing. All you really need it for is the cash drawer; you can log your sales on daily sheets of note paper. Good electronic cash registers are terribly expensive and cheap ones are junk. I think it's mostly esthetics; I like the old ones with a lot of brass and the sound of the bell when they're opened.

You'll need to establish a Visa & Mastercard retail account at your bank when you set up you company account. Don't even think about trying to be in business without the ability to accept these two major credit cards. I'd hate to think of all the big sales I'd have missed over the years without this system. And don't let them give you one of their big clumsy machines to print the vouchers with. They take up too much room and there's a monthly lease charge for them. For a one-time charge of ten dollars you can buy your own from your bank. It's flat, not much bigger than a check book, and works better. It also comes in handy later on if you begin to display at book fairs.

It is the custom among professional antiquarian booksellers to offer the protection of a mylar cover for the dust wrapper of any collectable hardback book. Personally I think anything over twenty dollars should have one. They are available from BRODART, INC. in a variety of sizes. You'll need mostly the ten inch size, with a smaller number of twelve and sixteen inchers. It makes quite a difference in the per unit cost if you can muster an order of one thousand so I always order eight hundred tens and a hundred each of the twelves and sixteens. It depends on how flush you feel; a thousand will last you two or three years but you're going to be around a long time.

BRODART also is the best source for those book mailers or "Jiffy Bags" you've probably seen offered for sale in your local Post Office. You won't need these right away but you will when you begin quoting so you might want to order some at the same time that you order the mylar covers. Ninety-five per cent of the books you'll ever need to ship will fit in the number 5 book mailer but you'll need some number 6's for folio-sized books as well.

Believe it or not, that's really about it. You'll need a handful of normal office supplies: ink pad, paper clips, etc. Don't forget to ask your bank to have a stamp made up for your store account and you make it a habit to stamp each check the moment you receive it. You'll want another stamp made up which looks like this:

Name: _____

Address: _____

Amount: _____

Date: _____

Buy a loose-leaf binder, fill it with unlined paper, and stamp the above in neat columns on the pages. Every time you buy books for cash you'll have the seller fill in his name, address and amount received. Not only does this give you an accounting of cash paid out, in some cities it's required by law. Some places, San Diego is one, place used book stores under the same restrictions as pawn shops so the above record is required. Whether it is or not where you set up shop it's a good idea just in case the issue ever arises as to the provenance of a book or books. The main reason, of course, is that it's the only record you have of the amount of cash paid out for books.

You'll want to pick up a simple receipt book. People sometimes request them when they are able to deduct the purchase of their books from their taxes. For the most part you will use it for writing up layaways. Many of your more expensive books will be sold on layaway and you'd do well to make an attractive sign offering this service to your customers. The normal deposit is anywhere from 20 per cent to a third down and the balance to suit the client — within reason. Set up a safe place in the back for your layaway books so they don't get picked up and sold inadvertantly. Never neglect to state a final balance due date on both copies of the receipt you make out. This way, if the book isn't redeemed by that date you may legally put it back in stock. If there is no final due date stated in the contract you may well be obliged to hold it forever. Give the original to the client and place the carbon inside the front cover of the layaway book.

All that remains is a trip to the printer. You'll want some attractive business cards made up. Look through the printer's book of logos and select something with class. I always use a logo of a shelf of very old-looking books, some lying flat and some standing upright. It appears on my cards, stationary and envelopes. You'll also want a supply of gift certificates; your printer will have several fancy formats to choose from. People like them to have a lot of scrollwork and they should be on good bond. They won't do you much good, however, if you don't find a conspicuous place to display one or two in your store. I place mine on a colored poster with the words ''Looking for the perfect gift?'' above the gift certificate and ''This is it!!'' below it.

7

Unravelling the Mare's Nest of Advertising

*One of the very interesting features of our times, is the
multiplication of books, and their distribution through all
conditions of society. At a small expense, a man can now
possess himself of the most precious treasures of English
literature. Books, once confined to a few by their costliness,
are now accessible to the multitude; and in this way a change
of habits is going on in society, highly favourable to the
culture of the people.*

W. E. Channing

NEVER HIDE YOUR LIGHT UNDER A BASKET WHEN IT COMES TO SIGNS

In the antiquarian book business there are very few ways of casting your
hard-earned bread upon the waters and getting anything back other than
soggy bread. The best possible use of your ad dollars is a sign. And I mean a
SIGN! The first store I ever owned was long established when I bought it.
It sported a two by four foot wooden sign with the name of the store carved
into it. On a clear day it was legible from maybe ten feet away if you had the
eyes of an eagle. The former owners were quite proud of it. They considered it subtle, exhibiting class but with restraint. They were right — it
was so subtle it was nearly non-existent. The store was averaging a hundred and thirty-four dollars a day in gross sales when I bought it. The first
thing I did was to take the sign home for firewood. The second was to order
a thirty-three foot long, three foot high illuminated sign reading,
"BOOKS, BOOKS, BOOKS." It was gold and featured black letters
nearly three feet tall and red and black books all over the sign. You could

see it from a mile away. Volume in the store doubled within two months. An incredible number of people began dropping in and saying something like, ''Did you just open?'' Some all but called me a liar when I told them the shop had been there for many years. ''But I walk past here almost every day and I never saw you before,'' they'd say. The fact is, people aren't all that observant. When I trained salesmen for 3M, I tried my best to impress this upon new men. I explained it thus: ''If you want to tell someone something, here's what you have to do. First you have to tell them you're going to tell them; then you have to tell them; and finally you have to tell them you told them.'' Laugh, but it's true. We're inundated with so much data today we walk around in pretty much a semi-concious state concerning everything which doesn't directly relate to our own self-interest.

My most recent store, which I opened in 1984, is set well back from the street in a small shopping center. It has a sixteen-foot lighted sign across the front but due to the setback and the sign's location parallel to the street, it blends in and gets lost among all the other stores' signs. A sign set at right angles to the street is worth ten set parallel to the street. So I rented one of those little portable signs on wheels and had it placed right out by the curb and at right angles to the street. It read ''BOOKS BOUGHT, SOLD & TRADED''. Business increased by somewhere between 30 and 40 per cent during the time this sign was in place.

The only problem was my lease limited me to no more than thirty days on a one time basis only, when it came to a portable sign. It seems the landlord thinks they're tacky and serve to diminish the grandeur of his complex. I intended to leave it there as long as I could but, sure enough, he called me on the thirty-first day and reminded me it was time to have the sign removed. I was in a real quandary. According to the terms of the lease, I could never again enjoy the terrific boost in sales the sign had created. I added an awning with an eighteen-inch by sixteen-foot sign on it but that didn't do much either because from the far-away street it was just another addition to the already confusing jumble of signs.

The answer was a simple one, as most truly satisfactory answers are. I bought an old VW Minibus and had five by ten foot vinyl panels made up for each side bearing the same message as had the smaller portable sign. Black letters on white vinyl — subtlety is not my bag. Every morning I'd park that van inside the curb at right angles to the traffic, right where the portable sign was. There are five grommets along the top of the panels; five ''S'' shaped hooks fasten into the grommets and catch over the little rain gutter running along the side of the roof. There's also a grommet at each of the lower corners where an elastic rubber cord with ''S'' hooks on each end pulls it tight by fastening it to the under-carriage.

A month after I began using the van signs my gross was up 50 per cent. That translates into a 100 per cent increase in the net profit. The van also comes in handy for picking up libraries. No, the landlord has never uttered a peep. What could he say? I moved the van every night and put it back in position every morning. Of course, it's no longer vital now that the shop is established but, as you can see, its effect was dramatic during the opening months.

There you have my basic treatise on signs. It's called do whatever you have to do. Have your signs painted with DAY-GLO or whatever. Just don't ever be afraid to shout your message to the world when it comes to signs. I once had a store where all you were allowed was one painted plywood sign mounted on the fascia of the building. I utilized every square inch available, black letters on a field of white again, then I installed a row of five hundred watt mercury vapor spotlights directed at the sign. I added a timer so that those spots came on every day at dusk. People kidded me, asking if I wasn't afraid an airplane wouldn't attempt to land on my roof some night. It was true; that sign shone like a beacon from among the maze of surrounding signs and when the spots came on in the evening it lighted the area until dawn. I once figured it out; the investment paid for itself every two and a half weeks.

HOW TO WASTE A TON OF MONEY ADVERTISING

You should be forewarned; as soon as you open a business you'll be inundated by salesmen selling everything from office supplies to insurance. But the vast majority of them will be peddling advertising of one kind or another. You'll be called upon by the reps from the local newspaper, the local free throw-away paper, the city magazine, all the local TV stations and the local radio stations. In addition, there will be the reps from the various companies which print handbills and distribute them to every household within a specified area around your business. (Sometimes they do; I once paid a sizeable fee for such a handbill, only to find the one person who redeemed the discount coupon it contained retrieved the flyer from a dumpster.)

The one thing all of these advertising media have in common is simply this: none of them work! I'm sure they work for many businesses but they won't do a thing for you. At least they never have for me and it's certainly not for lack of trying. You need to be told this and have it reinforced because you're vulnerable in the beginning and that's when all these vultures will descend upon you. I don't necessarily mean to demean them as a group but don't kid yourself; they're as slick as oiled ice. Salespersons flogging intangibles such as insurance and advertising have to be the very best in the business. It's all but impossible to listen to their pitch and not end up wanting to sign on the dotted line. I should know; I did it often enough, even long after I should have known better. But it's tough because they are so insidious, telling you what you long to hear at just the time you need to hear it the most. It's quite a nice ego stroke to hear your company's name blasted over the air waves but it's little more than that.

I don't think I've missed a bet when it comes to tossing away money on advertising. One of my stores was within a mile of San Diego State, a major university with well over thirty thousand students. A charming young lady — they mostly tend to be charming young ladies — convinced me my shop would be swarming with students if I would just buy an ad space on the free book covers the school handed out to the students at the school book store. She explained that the students were, as a group, voracious readers and represented the most promising segment of the population possible for a business like mine. The ad space was quite expensive but she capped the sale by guaranteeing me no other used book store would be allowed to buy space.

When one spends considerable sums of money on something like this you tend to keep track of the results. I accomplished this simply by stating in the ad that a twenty per cent discount would be given any State student who showed his student I.D. card. During the semester my ad was featured on the book jackets I had one young man ask for the discount; as I recall, it involved the sale of a dollar paperback. I later found out the covers were indeed available in the University book store but just sitting there, not being given out with book purchases. I also finally realized how few of the books being sold were hardbacks with dust wrappers.

Are you beginning to get my drift? Read on; I'm saving you thousands of dollars. Then there was the time I wrote the cutest comedy ad concerning a smart kid with a dumb dad cleaning their old books out of the attic. I laughed every time I heard it on the radio; it ran several weeks, five spots a day. That cost many times the price of the book covers but the results were the same. The ads were carried on a major station featuring light classical music, show tunes and standard hits — no country western or rock. The results were practically nil; I think one rather elderly couple said they heard the commercials and were curious. They admired the shop and left — empty-handed. It's taken me a long time to realize the obvious; readers read. They don't listen to commercials on radio or television, indeed they probably listen and view them far less than most. It's all a part of what advertisers refer to as the *Star Trek* Syndrome. When *Star Trek* was cancelled, in 1971 I believe, it was near the top of the ratings charts. It had been cancelled once before but was picked up again after the network supposedly received over one hundred thousand cards and letters urging the show remain on the air. That's a tremendous and totally unprecedented outpouring of support for a TV series, especially when you apply the standard formula of counting each letter as a hundred, the way network executives and sponsors do. Plenty of people were watching all right; the problem was they weren't buying the products. It's patently obvious some people can be manipulated by commercials and some cannot. I'm convinced most readers fall into the latter category.

I won't go into all my other follies, which include customized pens, calendars, bookmarks and mass mailings. It would be great if any of these gimmicks produced a fraction of what their promoters claim but they do not. It is not my intention to cast any aspersions upon these promoters; no doubt some of the success stories they claim are true. But it's one thing to pull customers into a grocery or clothing store and quite another to get them into an antiquarian book shop.

One of the very nicest things about this business is that you'll be dealing with a relatively small number of people, not the herds of folks needed to make most retail stores a success. Think about this: if you are open six days a week, eight hours a day, see an average of only six people an hour, each spending only ten dollars, you'll gross over twelve thousand dollars a month and should net six thousand dollars a month. It's just that simple!

SPEND A PITTANCE TO MAKE A MINT

The following are some ways in which the media may be used to the advantage of your shop.

Most daily newspapers will devote some space to new businesses. But you have to ask; they're not going to watch the new applications for business licenses and run you down as do the salesmen and promoters. They tend to be especially fascinated by interesting and unusual businesses like ours. If you promise them a nice shot of some fine bindings they're likely to dispatch a cameraman. TV stations usually don't respond but sometimes they do and it never hurts to ask.

A poster, perhaps with a picture of your shop's interior, listing the offering of your shop and its buying, selling and trading policies is one of the best selling tools I know of. Such posters are perfect for posting in teachers' lounges, for instance. Once you get a college or high school teacher in your shop you've pretty much won the battle. All you have to do is ask that they mention the shop to their students. It's amazing what lengths most people will go to in order to help you if only they are asked. Have you ever stopped to think how great it makes you feel to do someone a favor? Others like to enjoy that same warm glow. They will not only send you dozens of new customers, they will develop a proprietary feeling toward your shop which will make them go out of their way to insure your success. There are many ways in which they are able to do this, such as seeing that any really fine book offerings come your way.

Don't make up a hundred of these posters and run around placing them on bulletin boards in laundromats but use your imagination. Is there going to be a convention coming to town? Doctors, engineers, professional people generally tend to be collectors or at least readers. How about posting one at the site of your local PTA meetings?

Now I want to show you how to use the classified ads to increase your business. In spite of the sentiments voiced earlier in this chapter, I have found a way. If you have a choice between a daily newspaper and one of those free all-classified weeklies, elect the weekly every time. Those ads really get read and the edition isn't thrown out the next day when a new one arrives.

If you place an ad in there offering to sell books — no matter how cleverly you design it — I doubt it will do much good. Mine never did. But there's a bit of psychology that works like a charm. Put an ad in BEGGING people to SELL you books, pleading with them to come and take money from you. That they'll respond to with a vengeance. And if you word it right it's the greatest SELLING ad in the world. Use something on the order of: "HELP!! Top prices paid for your clean hardback and paperback books. Selling a thousand books a day and we need yours NOW!"

The beauty of it is, the ad indirectly delivers the message that something exciting is going on at your shop. Why are people buying a thousand books a day there? Your offering must be great and your prices fabulous. Book people will be compelled to come to see what all the excitement is about, whether or not they have any books they want to sell or trade. As for the claim of selling a thousand books a day, it will probably amount to about that soon after you open. They won't all be sales, perhaps half of that number will go out the door as trades, but it amounts to the same thing because you're delivering that many books to the public every day, on the average. If it sounds farfetched, all you have to do is picture a few ladies walking out the door with shopping bags full of Harlequins.

An ad like this is pure gold. Unlike most retail businesses you don't have to keep reselling your customers constantly. Once you've gotten them in the store they'll be yours for life. And, again unlike most other retail businesses, your sales aren't going to be a one-shot deal. If you sold refrigerators or cars you'd have to keep hammering at the public as long as you were in business. In the book business, you'll be dealing with the same clients regularly. After you've been in business for a while it shouldn't be necessary to run even the inexpensive little ad outlined above. The truth is, if you avoid the stupid mistakes I made in the beginning, it's going to be mighty tough finding ways to spend your profits.

There is one moderately-costly ad you cannot possibly do without — your local yellow pages. Not a day will go by when people in your area won't let their fingers do the walking. It's the first place they'll look when there is a library to be disposed of or an out-of-print book needed.

Gear your ad toward the sellers. This will attract buyers well enough, since it will indicate your only problem is keeping your shelves stocked. Use a heading like: TOP PRICES PAID FOR FINE LIBRARIES. It will entice every buyer and seller who sees it. Mention that you are open daily but never state the hours. This either restricts your ability to change or makes you a liar. Make it clear you are a full-range shop while listing your strong points or specialties, if any. Make certain your ad is equal or better to any other in the book. And make damn sure it appears under BOOKS, USED, not BOOKS, NEW. That happened to me one year, and while the phone company forgave most of the ad cost, it was a disaster of major proportions. Beware of ''ersatz'' yellow page directories offering lower-cost ads; you guessed it — they won't work for you either.

8

Open the Door and Let the Fun Begin

Books are the land where friendly people dwell,
he happy land where loved ones never die;
The young stay young, the old continue well,
Howe'er neglected in the dust they lie.
Within the pages born of human thought
We live again the battles men have fought,
And share their glad romances, old and new,
And tho we change, our books are always true.

Edgar A. Guest

PROPER FORMULA FOR TRADING BOOKS

Trading works pretty much the same from coast to coast. It's the best thing that ever happened to the antiquarian book trade. The great bonus is that it's wonderful for the consumer too. The principle is simplicity itself: you always trade two for one. You trade hardbacks for hardbacks; paperbacks for paperbacks. Now if every book was the same price all you'd have to do is count books. Unfortunately such is not the case. Therefore trades must be expressed in dollars rather than numbers of books.

Paperbacks are easy! You'll be selling them for one-half the publisher's original price on the cover so you'll credit the client bringing them in with one-quarter of that cover price. Ergo — a true two for one trade which is eminently fair to both parties. The way you do it is simply add up all the cover prices and divide by four and there you have the customer's trade value. Your retail value will, of course, be double that. In actual practice, someone might bring in six paperbacks, brand new ones with high cover prices, and walk out with a dozen older editions with low cover prices and have it work out to an even trade. Or conversely he might bring in a dozen and walk out with only two. It makes absolutely no difference to you the number of books involved either coming in or going out. You're doubling your money on every trade (assuming you're rejecting any unsalable books offered). When a client wants ten dollars worth of your books on trade he must bring you twenty dollars worth. That's twenty dollars worth of books you WANT, not just twenty dollars worth he wants to get rid of. You are going to be just as selective in accepting his books as he's going to be in choosing the books he wants to take out. Your customers will understand this as long as they see no junk being offered for sale on your shelves. We'll cover the parameters you'll be using to select your books in Chapter 9.

With hardbacks the principle remains exactly the same except that you won't be paying all that much attention to the publisher's original price. Even should the price be shown on the jacket it is not a useful guide to the value of that book in your store at that time. If it's a slow-moving subject — Architecture, say — the publisher's price might easily be $39.95. Experience will soon tell you that at anything over six dollars the book would probably sit on your shelf forever. Or you might have some old Americana book with a dust jacket price of $2.95 but you'll quickly come to know old, out-of-print Americana books move quickly for fifteen or twenty dollars easily. Enough on that until the following chapter.

So, the principle is the same but the difference is you must assign a value to each hardback as you total them on your machine. Believe me when I tell you it's a lot easier than it sounds and very soon becomes a matter of rote. The trick in the beginning is to do it without any outward show of indecision. Ambivalence will kill you in this business. I happen to believe firmly that ambivalence will kill you in life, but certainly it's true in the used book business. Like everybody else, I suppose, I've met a good many highly successful people. More than most perhaps because of the many collectors I've met and worked with. And I've met a lot of the other kind as well. I've trained myself to observe; when I trained salespeople, teaching them to really and truly observe was a large part of it. I'm convinced the one common denominator among all very successful people is the ability to make a decision quickly. If this is difficult for you, you're going to have a real problem running your shop. It's the only halfway difficult thing for assistants to become comfortable with when I'm breaking them in but after a couple of weeks they come to realize the earth isn't going to open up and swallow them if they make a mistake. And who knows what's a mistake?

No two booksellers going through a lot of twenty hardbacks or more will ever select exactly the same ones. It's absolutely true! I've tried the experiment many times with my wife, who loves working in the shop with me, and various assistants. There is always some variation in our respective selections. (Mine are always entirely correct, of course.) We all reject the obvious losers; that's not the problem. The discrepancy comes in because each of us will be attracted to some oddball title or subject the other has no interest in.

And I assure you the numbers are never going to come out the same either. This not an experiment you can conduct in front of the client but after they've gone, have someone else tally up a stack of hardbacks you've just accepted for trade or sale. The point is, there is no right answer, so quit worrying about it. Whip through those books, trust your gut instincts to select the right ones until experience takes over. Do it quickly, with authority, otherwise you invite debate. Just be certain if you err, and you will, do it on the side of the angels. (That's you.)

So now you've totaled the value of the hardbacks. If they're being offered for trade all you have to do is divide their retail value in two and you have the client's trade value. Why two instead of four as we did with the paperbacks? Because in the case of the paperbacks we were adding original publisher's prices which were DOUBLE what the books are to be sold for. In the case of hardbacks you are adding up your retail price, what you intend to sell them for, and thus you want to divide by two to arrive at a two-for-one trade value.

One of the most common mistakes made by so many book shops is imposing unnecesssary restrictions on their trades. I'm convinced an awful lot of people are born paranoid, or else they get it from the drinking water, and this is one of the manifestations. There are many shops which make you take out exactly the same subject matter you brought in for trade and that's ridiculous. I'll never forget hearing an anguished woman attempting to trade in such a store finally cry out, "Is it all right if I take different titles?" You will achieve the kind of success this book is all about if you keep one simple dictum in mind at all times: serve your customers as well as you possibly can. The rest is just mechanics.

Having said that, now I have to explain why it is necessary to impose some restrictions on trading. You will always trade fiction for fiction only. If they bring you non-fiction and want to take out fiction — terrific! That's a bonus! But fiction only gets fiction. The reason for that is simply the fact you can get in ten times as much fiction as nonfiction and if you don't impose this rule you'll quickly end up with a store full of fiction. Part of the problem is people consume a lot more fiction; they also are less likely to relinquish their good nonfiction.

The paperback for paperback and hardback for hardback rule is seldom a problem. In this case, nothing need be carved in stone if once in a while a steady customer asks for a favor. As you'll see shortly, you're paying the same rate for both types of book so it doesn't really hurt you a bit to let an occasional regular customer cross over. But you'll have a sign posted explaining your trading policies and I've very seldom had anyone ask for a dispensation.

There's only one more rule of trading I can think of and that's it. The whole idea, after all, is to keep it simple. (Always operate on the K.I.S.S. system — Keep It Simple, Stupid!) You may well have already anticipated it; Harlequins may only be traded for other Harlequins. The reason is obvious. In Chapter Six we went into how terribly common this genre is and the more common something is the more wary you'll have to be of becoming inundated with it.

There is a recent practice which seems to be gaining popularity around the country; it is the charging of a fee on all trades. The usual custom is to assess a ten cent charge upon each book being taken out of the store via trade credit. This is a dead giveaway to a failed shop. It is a desperate attempt to raise cash in those stores which have failed to establish sufficent volume of sales. True to the age-old proverb, they cut their noses off to spite their faces, giving their clients less, not more, reason to patronize them. These ''booksellers'' claim it is only fair for them to be reimbursed for their time and trouble in calculating trades and shelving the incoming books. What they fail to realize completely is the fact that they are totally dependent upon their wonderful customers for all stock and all sales. AND THEY WANT TO CHARGE THEIR CLIENTS FOR KEEPING THE SHOP IN BUSINESS! What it does, of course, is merely hasten the inevitable end. Given any other option, how long do you think your clients would tolerate paying you for the privilege of bringing you their best books?

The few rules above are all you'll want or need. They are simple enough for your customers to understand and not offensively restrictive. If a customer wishes to bring you Westerns and take out Mysteries, why not indulge him? In actual fact, the vast majority of people have well established reading patterns and will want to select from the same subject areas as the books they bring in for credit. In any event, you are always in complete control because each and every book you accept in trade you first have the opportunity to reject. I would estimate you'll find yourself passing on about two-thirds of the books brought to you for sale or trade. Much of this will be due to condition, some inappropriate subject matter — old textbooks, Reader's Digests, dated novels, outdated medical & legal guides, etc. — and the rest will be because you simply don't have a need for it right then. There will be times you will reject an offering but encourage the client to bring them back in two or three months; these will be nice saleable books which you just happen to be overstocked in at that moment.

Don't ever suffer from the dread that the source will be insufficient to keep up with the demand. It's a concern every used book dealer has agonized over in the beginning. You quickly get over it. Even the worst skinflint dealer — there are those who pay a dime for a paperback they sell for two dollars — doesn't have this problem. The fair and equitable way you are going to conduct your business will insure you will not only get more than your share of books, you'll soon be getting first choice while others will be offered mostly your rejects. No matter how successful you get, you'll always be offered far more books than you'll need.

You will need to set up a Trade Credit File. Get a file box that accommodates 3 x 5 cards and a set of alphabetical file dividers. Many of your customers will bring you large numbers of books for trade and not have the time or desire to use up all their credit on the spot. Many will simply get in the habit of dropping off boxes or bags of books in order to maintain a credit for the times they do choose to come in and browse for books. Write their names, last name first, and the date on one of these cards; then show the amount of their credit and the catagory that credit is in, (Fiction, Non-Fiction; hardback or paperback). I used to give these cards to the clients but they were forever losing them. I've never had anyone question the reliability of this system. You must arrive at an understanding, however, with those who wish to just drop off their books for future trade credit. They will probably not be new customers, but regulars, so they'll know the ropes. It is essential they agree to either pick up any rejects within say twenty-four hours or allow you the right to dispose of them. Your ability to store things like reject books is going to be minimal and you are doing this for their benefit, after all. If they are uncomfortable with such an arrangement, all they have to do is stand by while you cull through their books and take their rejects with them. This isn't usually a problem. Your clients come to trust you implicitly and they seldom have any desire to lug their rejects back home with them.

The reason for the date is interesting. There will come a time when you will go through the file and discard all credit cards showing no activity for a long period of time. I wait two years. You'll be amazed how many never use these credits. Just one more way your profit margin grows.

People will sometimes demand to know why you've rejected certain of their books. A polite, logical explanation will be accepted and appreciated. Your regulars soon learn to apply your standards themselves so there will be fewer and fewer culls from them. I must tell you about one notable exception to the rule about taking it well, however. I'd only been in business a couple of months when a wild-eyed woman of middle years rushed into my shop and BANGED her stack of books down on the counter. Every book was quite literally falling apart, so I informed her I would be unable to accept them due to poor condition. Well, she came completely unglued. She informed me in a loud strident voice she was a bona fide witch — this was indeed the subject matter of her books — and that there was now a curse upon my store. The shop was jammed with people at the time, some of whom were rolling on the floor holding their sides. As the woman rushed out the door she predicted I'd be bankrupt within a very short time. I guess she was having an off night though; business doubled over the next few months and I had to buy a hotel to keep my investment counselor from getting another ulcer.

PROPER FORMULA FOR BUYING BOOKS: BUYING PAPERBACKS

Buying paperbacks is simple. All you do is add the cover prices of the ones you've accepted and multiply by 12½ per cent. To express it another way: you're selling the books for half the cover price and you're buying them for 25 per cent of your retail. This also means you are awarding double the value in trade as you are in cash. I mentioned earlier the vast majority of clients will elect to trade; now you know why. If they sold their books, then turned around and used the money to buy books, they'd be paying double.

Nothing could be more straightforward but, as in most things, there are likely to be exceptions. It's hard for me to predict in advance just what those exceptions might be in your part of the country, so let me give you the ones I've made as examples. I told you earlier that Science Fiction and Fantasy was the most difficult section for me to fill in the beginning. I finally solved this problem in three ways. I bought a small beginning nucleus of titles from another dealer because you can't build a section by trading until you've got SOMETHING to trade. Secondly I paid a premium price of 15 per cent of the cover price instead of the standard 12½ until the section was healthy. After that I dropped back to the lower figure. Thirdly, I merely asked people to bring me Science Fiction. When you see a customer making a purchase from a section you wish to build, ask him if he wouldn't consider bringing in any of his duplicates or titles he may not want to read again. The response will warm your heart.

The various fiction sections, with the possible exception of Science Fiction as noted above, will be the first to get healthy. When that begins to happen, drop your cash price for fiction down to 10 per cent. There's no point in paying as much for fiction as nonfiction; the fact is, you'll soon be buying almost no fiction paperbacks at all. Long after you've stopped buying novels, romances and mysteries, you may still be willing to buy Westerns and Fantasy. I've never seen a day when I wasn't willing to buy Fantasy, but this will be the exception and not the rule.

This leaves you with an established policy of paying premium prices for nonfiction. You should let your clients know that; it will make them feel more inclined to bring you the precious nonfiction books you need.

BUYING HARDBACKS

When buying hardbacks, you're faced with the same need to run quickly through the ones you've decided are suitable and to tally them up on your machine. As with trading, you'll be utilizing YOUR RETAIL values here as opposed to publishers' prices. When you arrive at a subtotal, all you have to do is multiply by 25 per cent and there you have the cash price you should pay for that lot of books.

The above formula covers 99 per cent of your cash transactions when buying hardbacks. We must now devote some time to the remaining one per cent. It's always been my policy, and I believe it's proven a sound one, to pay from 25 to 50 per cent of my retail for hardback books. When clients ask me in the store or call on the phone that's exactly what I tell them. I go on to explain the lower figure is for common material and the highest figure is for scarce or rare books. And that is exactly what I do pay, but the point is it somehow puts the onus on the client to come up with superior material if he wants the premium price. It serves to tell collectors and people who have unusually desirable books that you're not going to treat them as you would the guy with a box full of Book-Of-The-Month-Club books. And this is a message you must project if you ever want to upgrade your shop and make it a truly fine antiquarian store.

Very little of the material brought to you will warrant the 50 per cent premium (You'll always wish there were more of THIS coming in) but never hesitate to pay it when it does. You'll be tested; if you don't pay a fair price, there won't be any more forthcoming from that source. But pay the top price only for top stock in prime condition. We're talking about signed first editions, limited editions, illustrated books bound in vellum, collectable editions of works by important authors with wrappers intact, seventeenth and eighteenth century books on interesting subjects in very good condition. Never be foolish enough to invest heavily in first editions or signed material by authors nobody cares about. Remember very few are sought; I've sold thousands of signed first editions by also-ran writers for two or three dollars and was delighted to do so.

Much more common that anything falling within the premium price range will the middle ground material where you should pay thirty-five per cent of retail. You should be happy to do so because there are hundreds of times as many prospective clients for this stock as there are collectors for the top-of-the-line books. This middle ground consists of sets of *Britannica III*, the *Great Books of the Western World*, any literary sets which are complete and in unusually attractive bindings, just about any books bound in full calf, sets of Durant's *Making of Civilization*, big beautiful art books by such outstanding publishers as Abrams, you get the idea. Usually books in slipcases deserve to fall into this category, though not always. My test is an easy one: if my first impression is I'd like to take it home myself, then it deserves the higher price.

Very often there will be only two or three such books in a lot of otherwise average books. Rather than have to add them separately, it's a simple matter to just assign them slightly higher values when you punch them into the machine so that using the lower percentage still comes out equitably.

PRICING GENERAL STOCK

Here the motto is: KEEP IT CHEAP! Just about the dumbest thing you could do is to price your common hardbacks right up to the roof and then sit there and watch them get dusty as you turn down multiple copies of the same material regularly. Doesn't it make a hell of a lot more sense to price the easy stuff way down low and keep selling and replacing it? What's better? To sell one copy for ten dollars in three years and have the client resent the fact you charged him that much? Or to sell fifteen or twenty copies for three or four dollars in three years and have gained the respect and loyalty of your buyers? (I give easy tests, don't I?)

I know it sounds simplistic but most of the shops in the country operate on the former principle. It makes me crazy, but they do. And they wonder why their stores are so empty.

The real secret of this business is turnover. If you can just grasp that one fact, you'll be fine. Turnover makes everything else work. If you keep it cheap, you'll move the books. If you move the books you'll be able to accept the new material constantly being offered to you. If you are able to accept new material, your regulars — the ones who are the key to your success — will never become bored with your store and your stock. You begin to see how the whole thing progresses almost geometrically? It is NEVER the idea to get a better price for your books than the other guy; the idea is to sell as much as you possibly can in order to keep your stock eternally fresh and interesting. Please write that on the blackboard one hundred times or whatever works for you so that it is emblazoned upon your mind.

And never let a book grow too stale on your shelves. Never mind what you paid for it; if it's still there a year later it's costing you far more than what you paid for it. It's become many things — all negative.

You'll come to know your books remarkably well. It always amazes customers when someone calls on the phone requesting a book and you immediately know whether or not you have it in stock. But when you buy it, price it and shelve it, you know it's there. The point is, if it remains there for too long, it's time to do something different. Remember, we're speaking of general stock right now, not collector's items.

The most innocuous thing you can do is to refile it in another section. A prime example would be a copy of Herman Wouk's *Winds of War*. Say you've been looking at a copy in the WAR: FICTION section for six months and it's beginning to have that stale look you want to avoid. (This is one of the few advantages the new book store has over you; all they have to do is return it to the publisher or wholesaler.) You might move it to general fiction. Even better, move it to classics. Writers such as Wouk, who are a bit too literate for the average reader, usually sell very well in classics where buyers are looking for a little more of a challenge. It is always a good idea to spread a title around when you find yourself with multiple copies. I can assure you you'll do better to have one copy of a given title in three different sections than to have all three sitting together.

The following general guidelines should be helpful when it comes to pricing your general hardback stock. Fiction is going to be less than non-fiction. Hardback novels should begin at two dollars and not go much over three except for titles which are still on the Best Seller list and perhaps extra-long books for which there is a strong demand such as Michener's. In other words, sell them like hamburger — by the pound. As you log time in the business in your area you will be better able to gauge which authors are in demand. Local authors who write of local settings will always be hot.

Genre fiction pricing is generally the same, as long as we're concerned with in-print titles. We'll deal with out-of-print titles later in this chapter. It is the current custom of some publishers to reprint classic material in the mystery, science fiction, classic and other subjects in omnibus volumes. These usually contain three full-length works but may contain as many as five books. You mustn't feel you can multiply the price you would put on a single title times the number of titles within the omnibus volume. These books are invariably designed to sell inexpensively, (One reason being the material has often become public domain.) And don't be fooled by the ersatz leatherlike bindings. Nothing embarrasses me more than to walk into a used book store and find one of these contemporary omnibuses with the leatherlike plastic binding being offered as a collectable for twenty-five dollars while there are pyramids of the same book at the local new book store priced at under nine dollars. It happens all too frequently. This is a good time to reinforce my earlier enjoinder to visit the new shops in your community often. It is essential you know what books are being ''remaindered.'' This is a term used to describe books which are being sold new for a fraction of their dust wrapper price. They may be books for which the market was overestimated, but for whatever reason they have been drastically reduced in price by the publisher. Due to a change in the tax laws a few years back, publishers are no longer able to warehouse these books and use them as a tax loss, so there are a lot of bargains in the new shops these days. It would not be unusual to see books with publishers' prices of $29.95 being offered new at $9.95. A common sight just a few years ago, after the death of famed illustrator Norman Rockwell, was that of folio-sized books of his works for sale in used shops for double what they were going for new. It's one of the best ways I know to advertise to your customers either you don't know what you're doing or you're trying to rip them off. I don't think either is going to help your cause.

Nonfiction is tougher to generalize about. It is certainly safe to state that prices will be somewhat higher than with fiction. The rule, most simply stated, is: supply and demand dictate price. Local Americana will sell for much more in any given store anywhere than will gardening or sports books. Again, the hamburger principle applies; books actually do tend to sell by the pound if they are contemporary, in-print titles. You'll soon develop your own list of "hot" subjects and you'll push prices within these areas in order to balance the ebb and flow of this material.

There should be few nonfiction books on your shelf for under three dollars. It's impossible to engrave such statements in stone because there'll always be the odd thin little volume among the cookbooks or wherever which just doesn't merit it but they should be few and far between. The range for fairly common nonfiction titles still in print will pretty much be from three to five dollars.

This does NOT mean you are going to offer beautifully bound books currently costing thirty to one hundred dollars for five dollars. But such books are easily recognized. Books concerning art, architecture, some references, some cookbooks, others will bear a higher price; they will speak to you and you must trust your instincts. When pricing your more expensive books, I believe it's a good idea to write I.P. — in print — followed by the new retail price. Then draw a line through this price and beneath it write your price. Nothing could more dramatically illustrate the savings you are offering. As a general rule, your price should be approximately one third of the full retail price of an in-print book. Half is the more common rule throughout the industry but pricing your in-print hardbacks at half is a foolish, expensive mistake you'd do well to avoid.

If you're still looking at them a year later, slash the price. I mean that quite literally. Line out the old price and write in the new one beneath it. We all love to know we're buying something for less than the full or original price. I slash prices all the time and it's a common occurrence for those books I reduce to sell quickly. Many a client has brought one to the counter and told me, ''I've had my eye on this book for a long time but I just couldn't justify the price. I'm so happy to see you've reduced it.''

PRICING OUT-OF-PRINT BOOKS

This section could easily constitute a book in itself but in the end all anyone can give you are some general guidelines and encourage you to trust your gut.

First it's essential to establish the fact that, just because a book is out of print, it isn't necessarily valuable. Quite the contrary; roughly 90 per cent of the out of print titles are entirely worthless. This is especially true of fiction but God knows the world is full of O.P. nonfiction which is worthless as well. (From now on I will be using the designations O.P. and I.P. for out-of-print and in-print).

Lesson number two is to get into the invariable habit of writing O.P. in front of your pricing on any out-of-print book. The client needs to know whether a book is O.P. or not; it may well make the difference whether or not he buys the book. If he believes it to be still in print — readily available whenever it suits him — he may well elect to put the purchase off. If your copy is less than fine he may decide to order a new one unless you let him know it is O.P.

In order to know whether or not a book is still in print you will need a Bowker's BOOKS IN PRINT. There are two sets, one referenced by title and the other by author. Address of the publisher may be found in Chapter 18. In actual practice, I have always found these books at library sales or at other book shops. It isn't vital you have the current edition.

Factors which you will wish to take into account when judging any O.P. book are first of all condition. Probably the single most common failing I find when I walk into the average antiquarian book shop is garbage on their shelves justified by the reverently-uttered explanation, or perhaps a sign, that those books are O.P. So what? They're O.P. garbage. If anything, you should be more demanding when it comes to more expensive material because collectors are a mighty fussy bunch. Obviously you make adjustments for time; you'd accept a more worn copy of an eighteenth century book than you would one published in 1950. But please never put books out with chipped spines or missing backstrips; you only do yourself and your shop a grave disservice. If you ever find yourself in possession of a truly valuable tome, intact but in horrible condition, keep it in the back until the right buyer comes along.

Here's where we come up against an age-old dispute within the antiquarian book industry: to rebind or not to rebind, that is the question. It's a simple matter to have a valuable book rebound in leather or buckram and end up with a handsome product. The trouble is, anything you do to change a collectable book from the original decreases its value. The logical compromise is to leave it alone and let the collector who buys it decide the issue. If you must do a rebind on an antiquarian book, at least have the binder affix the original label, if there is one, onto the new spine and lay in as much of the original covers and spine as remains inside the front cover.

There is an invaluable tool for the bookseller called the *Antiquarian Bookman,* usually referred to as the AB. It is published weekly, fifty times a year, and a subscription to it is a must. One of the things it will do for you is educate you as to what books are currently in great demand. Most of the periodical is given over to ads from dealers from all over the United States and foreign countries soliciting books for which they have buyers. Through reading these ads you'll quickly gain a feel for what is truly scarce and desirable. Details for subscribing to the AB may be found in Chapter 18. I would encourage you to do so even if you're uncertain about whether or not you want to open your own shop or if the time is yet some distance off. Reading the ads and editorials will gain you an ever-increasing depth of knowledge concerning this industry.

So you're going to price O.P. books on the basis of content, age and condition. Hot subjects range from circus material to weaponry and Americana. Nineteenth century and older science books are sellers. Books of little interest in spite of their antiquity are mainly religious in nature. The farther back you go, the greater was the percentage of books devoted to religious studies, so always remember there's nothing nearly so common as an old Bible. What was the one book every child was certain to get as a gift every time he graduated, married or accomplished anything calling for a gift? You got it — a Bible. I don't mean to say a fine hand-tooled leather-bound Bible from the seventeenth or eighteenth century is unsaleable — it isn't. It's just that it's the one subject which is monotonously common among old books and therefore among the least valuable.

If indeed the old Bible referred to above has real value, it will be predicated upon the binding, not the contents. This holds true for any old book; their value often determined as a work of art, in spite of and not because of the contents.

You must not jump to conclusions, however. Up until near the end of the eighteenth century, nearly all books assumed a cloak of religiosity according to custom. They often began something like, "To the everlasting glory of God and with homage to the King. . ." even though they might be books on anything from astronomy to gardening. By the way, if you've never acquired a working knowledge of Latin, you really must get a primer and at the very least learn to read the publication dates. The bulk of material pre-eighteenth century is going to be in Latin and even if it's in another language the date is likely to be in Latin. It isn't necessary you be able to speed-read the book but you will need to be able to ascertain the date and the subject matter.

Just as a general guideline, any good O.P. book should be worth more than the average I.P. book. Simple availability dictates this should be so. How much more is a matter of experience and instinct. In most cases, the answer will be, not one whole hell of a lot. You'll have a lot more customers looking for the latest Michener or King title than you will a hundred year old book on building an earthen dam. But the point is this: the latest Michener and King titles are available everywhere including drug and department stores. They must be sold on the basis of price. That old book on dams is your exclusive and when the appropriate buyer sees it he's going to consider it in an entirely different light. He's going to have to decide whether or not he ever wants to own that book, knowing full well he'll probably never see another copy. Price is still a factor, yes, but no longer the primary one.

The price range on clean, interesting O.P. books should begin around five dollars. If I had to guess, I'd say the average price of an O.P. book in any one of my stores would be twelve dollars. A great many would be five and and quite a few would be fifty dollars. Anything over that comes under the heading of collectable, which is the final section in this chapter.

Your standards will be slightly relaxed when it comes to O.P. books. Interesting titles will be accepted in spite of missing dust jackets. A bit more rubbing at the corners and shelf wear and fading will be tolerated with each added year if the material is of merit. Don't waste shelf space on old medical books or bound periodicals such as J.A.M.A. (Journal of the American Medical Association.). Old law books are as worthless. Other than that, go with what seems reasonably interesting to you. Your customers will make their wants known soon enough, telling you what to watch for.

O.P. fiction is easier; it will take you very little time to discover what authors are in demand and how heavy-handed you can get with your pricing. In my experience, the following authors head the list: Gene Stratton Porter, E.R. Burroughs, Jack London, H.P. Lovecraft and the list goes on. Classics, by their very definition, will always be in demand. There are also a great host of so-called ''popular'' authors for which the market remains strong. There are a great many collectors in the world attempting to complete runs of every book written by some favorite author. The longer the books have been O.P. the more difficult the task becomes. In many cases the books may still be in print in paperback but this doesn't alter the fact that the hardback is O.P. and perhaps scarce. E.R. Burroughs is a fair example. Most of his titles remain I.P. in paperback format but his hard-backs have been O.P. for nearly a decade. Collectors may buy a paperback as a temporary measure, but only until a nice hardback becomes available. Less than two decades ago, Burroughs had the distinction of being the most widely published fiction writer in history, so obviously there is no shortage of his books around. And yet within the last ten years I've watched his hardback reprints climb from a few dollars to as much as seventy-five dollars in the case of some of his old Grosset & Dunlap editions with original dust wrappers. Bear in mind I'm not talking about first editions, just sharp reprints in nice wrappers.

The above example holds true for many another author from the past. James Oliver Curwoood, H.B. Wright, Zane Grey, the list is long and interesting. Here again, your section of the country will determine the special emphasis your O.P. stock should reflect. Example: in Southern California I used to put Harold Bell Wright titles on the shelf for two or three dollars and hope for the best. There was little or no interest in the preachy romances. But when I opened up in the Ozarks I found it impossible to keep up with the demand for Wright material. I let my pricing inch upward until I achieved some semblance of balance between supply and demand. Wright spent part of his life here in Ozark country and his simplistic morality plays have great appeal in the Bible Belt.

You'll soon note the ads in the AB verifying this regional demand. Dealers in the South plead for Southern authors and in the Southwest they cry for writers like J. Frank Dobie. This phenomena is one of the major reasons for the constant flood of books back and forth across the country. It also explains how an antiquarian dealer is able to meet his clients' needs and make a profit. Books worth little in one section are often quite valuable in another. If you utilize your subscription to the AB wisely you will become a part of this pipeline, to the delight of both your clients and your accountant.

PRICING COLLECTABLE BOOKS

Before you can price a collectable book you have to be able to recognize one. Your weekly perusal of the AB will solve that problem nicely. It won't take you long to figure out a fine first edition of Hemingway is worth something and a fine first of Joe Doaks is not.

The next thing you have to learn is how to grade a collectable book. The value of a first or limited edition will vary widely according to grading; there are really only five grades commonly used.

Reading copy: means just that. It's OK to read if nobody's watching. Pages are intact but condition is awful.

Good: this allows for relatively minor defects such as shelf wear, rubbing, slight soiling or fading but nothing as serious as chipped spine or broken hinge. Not good enough for most collectors unless we're talking about truly scarce antiquarian material.

Very good: must be a tight, nearly unblemished book but perhaps one which has lost that crisp feel and luster a new book has. Wear must be very minor, if any.

Fine: self-explanatory. No defects of any kind.

Mint: an unused copy yet to be cracked open. Stiff hinges. Perfect as issued.

Strict grading is a virtue to be sought. It will endear you to your peers or, conversely, irritate the hell out of them. When pricing your collectable books be conservative with your grading and be prepared to knock off substantial amounts from the Fine price quoted in your reference if yours is only VG. A good rule of thumb for twentieth century first editions is to reduce the Fine price by one-third for a VG copy. A Good only copy should be filed in with general stock and not even considered a collectable. Pre-twentieth century you begin to make allowances on pricing. Your grading should remain as strict but there are going to be damn few Fine copies of an early nineteenth century first edition so you will accordingly make much less of a price reduction for a VG copy.

It will be necessary for you to obtain one or more of the current price guides. No doubt your local library has some, but you can't be bothered chasing over to use theirs every other day. There are several references; you will find addresses listed in Chapter 19.

If you want to get by cheaply in the beginning, Van Allen Bradley's *Handbook of Values** will get you by for a while. It is a not very comprehensive one-volume price guide and its values tend to get beginners into trouble. Some prices are sky high, such as Rackham illustrated books, and some are ludicrously low, like firsts of Ray Bradbury and some other fantasy writers. It does give a good description of "points"—the errors or deviations which indicate a true first—and that's really what you need a reference for.

Used Book Price Guide is a three-volume set which I like very much except for the fact that its prices are very conservative. Volume three is a later supplement and you can get by without it if need be but volumes one and two are each only half of one book so you'll need them both.

Bookman's Price Index is another excellent set. I like volume one because it has quite a few periodical values. This set is up to about volume twenty now, I believe, but each volume stands on its own so any of them would be helpful.

American Book Prices Current is favored by many dealers because the prices tend to be higher oftentimes. As with the others, prices given are those realized at actual auctions. If you stop to think that most books sold at auction are bought by dealers for resale, the prices in the references should be somewhat low.

The above price guides all tend to be quite expensive, with the exception of Bradley's *Handbook of Values*. Frankly, I have never found it necessary to buy any of them new; yet I've managed to accumulate all of them. Some will come to you along with all the other wonderful books you'll acquire once your doors are open. You'll find them at library sales and should never miss an opportunity to attend one. You will see them offered by other dealers in the AB. Never hesitate to buy any of the above price guides regardless of the vintage. You need them far less as time goes by for price references than you do for "points." It is often next to impossible to determine whether a given book is truly a first edition or a reprint without a reference giving you the "points" to look for. Usually it's an error in spelling or a broken piece of type—some glitch which was removed in subsequent printings. Sometimes it's the binding; red cloth is a first, blue is a

Editor's note:

*Out of print at time of this edition. Please check Chapter 19 for updated reference sources.

second, even though everything else on the title and the verso page remains the same. It can even be a change in the dedication or, in the case of one of Hemingway's titles, the lack of a credit to the photographer who did the cover photo of the author. You begin to get the idea? You'll come to know prices well enough for much of your collectable stock but there will never come a day when you won't need references to find out whether or not you actually have a first edition.

Most libraries I've checked had a copy of H. S. Boutell's *First Editions of Today and How To Tell Them*. When I was starting out I merely photocopied this fine reference right in my friendly neighborhood library and I'm still using those original sheets, fastened in a clipboard, to this day.

These days there's a better way, however. For twenty dollars you can buy a hardback reference entitled, *First Editions: A Guide To Identification*. This excellent value covers over one thousand publishers; it is put out by The Spoon River Press. It's probably less expensive to buy this book than it would be to photocopy Boutell. Unfortunately, this valuable reference wasn't available yet when I started out.

Sometimes it almost seems as if some publishers deliberately obscure their first printings. Nowadays many such as Random House clearly state "First Edition" on the copyright page but this is more the exception than the rule. Others like Viking publish a history of previous printings so that no statement on the verso page indicates a first. Some, Holt Rinehart for example, placed their colophon on the copyright page for the first printing, removing it for subsequent printings. Scribners currently inserts an "A" on the verso page to indicate a first printing but prior to 1939 they weren't so considerate.

Those above are the easy ones. Now it's necessary for me to muddy the waters even more by warning you that not all books which state "First Edition" on the copyright page are indeed firsts. Some reprint publishers bought the plates from the original house and ran off inexpensive reprints which still bore the first edition statement. Even today it is not uncommon within the Science Fiction/Fantasy genre for classic titles to be reprinted as stated firsts. Usually these reprints may be distinguished by a difference in the binding, known as "binding states" but only if you've got a good reference and the good sense to use it.

The most common contemporary "non-first" is the stated first edition that is a book club edition. You'll see a lot of these so pay particular attention to the following. Publishers sell a lot of books to book clubs; the major houses even have their own clubs. Now most book club editions are printed specifically for that club and are easily recognizable. They are bound in cheap resin-impregnated boards with poor quality paper and are physically smaller, thinner and a lot lighter than the publisher's edition. They bear no price in the usual place at the upper right of the dust wrapper panel just inside the front cover. No problem; you'll quickly be able to tell a book club the moment you pick it up. It's common for me to be going through a batch of book clubs and, noting the weight of one book as I lift it, to state, "This one isn't a book club."

The problem is some of the books sold through clubs are nice cloth bound editions stating "FIRST EDITION" clearly on the verso page. But no collector will ever be fooled, so train yourself to automatically make the following checks. Is there a price on the dust wrapper? If not, you probably are holding a book club edition. The fact that it may be a stated first makes no difference whatsoever. A first must be in a first issue dust wrapper. When publishers sell their overruns to book clubs the clubs print up their own dust wrappers and put them on the books. It will be identical in every way except for the deletion of the publisher's price on the front panel.

Make one more check if there's no price. Remove the rear panel of the dust jacket and take a close look at the bottom right of the back cover. In every case — if it's a book club edition — there will be a small mark impressed upon the binding. It may be a tiny circle or a square or the logo of the original publisher, but it will be there. This is the one final and absolute way in which you can always identify a book club. The most common example of this one sees today is Michener's titles published by Random House. I know I've been offered dozens if not hundreds of stated firsts which were book clubs. What's the difference? It's true the books are the same in every way as the actual firsts except for the missing price on the wrapper and that tiny impressure mark on the back cover. The difference is this: one is worth in excess of its original publisher's price the moment it goes into reprint (meaning you can no longer get firsts from the publisher.) and the other is nothing but a reading copy and never will be anything more.

This completes my brief dissertation on the pricing of collectable books. It's a subject upon which there is ample room for men of good will to disagree. Much depends upon locality, personal interests and the swing of the pendulum of faddishness. Don't try going for the jugular when pricing even your finest material. The principal remains the same as with both general stock and out-of-print books. The idea isn't to see how much you can get for any given book. The idea is to convert the book back into cash and reinvest it again and again, etc. (You get the idea.)

Just so you'll know the antiquarian book trade is not without its characters, there's the classic and I don't think entirely apochryphal story about the dealer who goes to great lengths to acquire all the copies he can of a specific scarce title. He then goes to an auction and deliberately bids a copy, perhaps with the help of an accomplice, to a figure several times its true value. He then uses that auction record to justify the prices he gets for the other copies.

So auction prices are all well and good, but try and cross-reference them with another source. Never offer an opinion on a book unseen; it can only serve to embarrass you later. And get used to the idea that most old books are of little value, even though they may be a couple of hundred years old and in VG condition. (Eighteenth century theology books, for instance, are a dime a dozen.)

I have avoided going into the subject of pricing collectable paperbacks for several reasons. Unless you are located in a very large metropolitan area it is likely to hurt you more than help you. Unsophisticated customers will resent seeing a paperback with a twenty-five cent cover price in a plastic baggie marked five dollars. You will find a guide for pricing many of these books listed in Chapter 19 entitled *Official Price Guide To Paperbacks and Magazines*.

If you are interested, the most sought-after are the early Ace publications, Ace Doubles (two books in one binding), Dell Mapbacks (mysteries with maps of the setting on the back) and books based on old TV series (Man From U.N.C.L.E. for instance).

There is also a brisk market for old pulps such as Weird Tales, Wonder Stories and Black Mask. Such material should always be displayed in plastic bags, both to protect and to let non-collectors know they are exempt from your usual pricing policy. The above-mentioned price guide also covers such material.

9

Secret of Maintaining a Quality Offering

By the very nature of their occupation booksellers are broad-minded; their association with every class of humanity and their constant companionship with books give them a liberality that enables them to view with singular clearness and dispassionateness every phase of life and every dispensation of Providence.

Eugene Field

CONDITION IS ALL-IMPORTANT

The single most depressing thing I see over and over again when I travel around the country is the sight of valuable shelving being wasted on totally unsaleable books. Not only is it disastrous to stock books nobody wants, the sight of such stock imparts a clear message to those who come into your shop. It tells them you are an amateur. It tells them your instincts are lousy. It tells them you couldn't care less about your clients. And it tells them there is little likelihood another visit would prove rewarding.

I've seen too many shops in which I swear the owner would do himself and his customers a great favor if he'd trundle half of his stock down to the nearest Salvation Army and donate it. There are literally thousands of stores in this country heavily stocked with books which are water-stained, books which reek of mildew, books with chipped spines and broken hinges, and books which are so filthy I can't imagine anyone even contemplating picking them up. There is only one excuse for this — an irresistible urge to go bankrupt. Some of these stores actually earn a fine living for their owners but that's only because their poor clients have no other options. Establish a decent shop in that town and there'll soon be a building for rent.

Any given book is either saleable or it's garbage. Obviously the ones described above are garbage. A good example is book club novels by less-than-major writers. You'll always be offered fifty times the numbers you need so there is no reason on earth to ever take one which is anything but mint. Think about it; there are only two ways to find out what an unfamiliar novel is about. One is to read the panels inside the dust jacket and the other is to read the book. There are some instances I can think of where it is advisable to take fictional hardbacks without dust wrappers but these are exceptional. Michener, Stout, MacDonald, Christie, Chandler, Hammet, Wouk, King and others, but as a general rule don't do it. You'd clearly understand what I mean if you could walk into a store which follows this policy and see all those bright and colorful jackets arrayed upon the shelves. Or next time you are near a new book shop, step inside and visualize it with all or even some of the wrappers removed. Much of the beauty, charm and allure would be gone, don't you see. There's nothing duller than a shop with shelves loaded with unwrapped novels. They appear drab and worn, often faded so that you can't even tell what the book is without removing it from the shelf. I can tell you from hard-won experience, no one ever will take it from the shelf to find out. Such a store always looks as if all the books should be priced three for a dollar. And that's not the image you will want to project. The idea is to make all your books look as if they are worth plenty and have the client be pleasantly surprised when he finds out how reasonably you've priced them.

I've walked into stores where the stench of mildew hit me like a wall. I've seen books with their covers held on with tape. I've seen books offered for sale with rubber bands around them to secure loose pages. And, as God is my witness, I saw one store where they offered books with up to half the pages missing but at a suitable discount. Can you believe it? Now do you begin to appreciate why there is a huge demand for fine, well-run shops all across this country?

In this business we all greatly prize fine old leatherbounds but still the same principles apply. It's true you will want to make some allowances for a two hundred year old book or more but there's still a point at which such material is garbage. Slight chipping of the spine, perhaps shaken hinges and normal rubbing — shelf wear — is acceptable, but not missing pages or plates or detached boards or half the spine missing.

When it comes to nonfiction, that's a little different. If the subject material is hot or the author scarce, go for it. But you still have to have a legible title on the spine. If you can't tell what it is once it's on the shelf it will disappear completely and you may as well not have it. It's one of the most frustrating things in the business to have to pass up good stock merely because the title is completely faded from the spine but you'll be better off to grit your teeth and do it. I will make an exception if it's a really gangbusters title but then I have to display it either on the shelf or in the window face out so people can see what it is.

Rough paperbacks are even more inexcusable than hardbacks. To place shabby, dog-eared or dirty paperbacks on your shelves is surely the height of stupidity. Your regular pocket book buyers — the ones who pay your rent — will certainly not pay you even half the cover price for such material, nor will they bring you their clean, sharp books for trade and take out crap. Perhaps you feel even rough books have some value and should be stocked and sold but at less than half cover. I've seen many shops doing just that. I've never seen what I refer to as a successful shop doing that on a regular basis. Perhaps an occasional sale but not routinely. Such a store is entirely different from the kind of fine general stock antiquarian shop this book is devoted to. If you want to compete with the thrift stores — who are given their books free, don't forget — and sell your paperbacks for twenty-five cents, fine. But good luck on ever being taken seriously as a fine book shop and making more than slave wages.

Remember, you and your shop will be judged every time someone steps through the door. All your paperbacks should be very nearly as new. It's no problem; you'll be turning away tons of them soon after you open. The one noteworthy exception will be westerns. You'll have to give a little on those or you'll never have enough but everything else should be sharp.

Develop the habit of fanning through the pages of the first few books in a lot you are buying or trading for. Look for underlining or highlighting. Never accept any book which is so defaced. If you've ever tried to read a book someone else has marked up you'll know how maddening it is.

If you get in a desirable book but with a torn dust jacket, fine, just take a few seconds before putting it on the shelf to repair the wrapper with a small amount of Scotch tape. On the inside, of course. Check your shelves as you are putting up stock. If a book begins to look shopworn, do something about it. Repair the wrapper. Perhaps it's a matter of reducing the price or maybe it's time to place it on the bargain rack. Do something; don't just let it sit there looking increasingly shabby. Once an asset turns into a liability, get rid of it quickly.

Start picky and stay that way. Your customers will admire you for it and show their appreciation in a very tangible way. Those who bring you only shabby books might well be satisfied to buy or trade for shabby books but these you may do well to lose to a competitor. Over the years some of my best customers told me until they discovered my store they would have taken an oath they'd never be caught dead in a used book store. I've also had people come into my shops and walk around before coming up to the desk and telling me they have a fine library for sale but this was the first shop they'd seen worthy of having their books. Junk begets junk; quality is self-regenerating. Such people had only seen stores which were dirty and didn't smell too good, where the books were mostly like the ones at Salvation Army for fifty cents. Operate a class act and your biggest problem in life will soon be to find a really good tax man.

BOOKS WHICH WILL COST YOU MONEY

There are certain categories of books which always betray the unskilled amateurs in this business. They not only won't sell, they rob your shop of its stature and credibility. It should be no surprise to learn these books are exceedingly common; that's one of the major reasons they must be avoided at all costs. Place a value on every running inch of your shelving and make damn sure every book to which you allot some valuable space deserves the privilege.

The following is a partial list of types of books which do not deserve space. Reader's Digest Condensed Books. (Please note this does not include Reader's Digest nonfiction publications, most of which are very desirable.) Nearly all textbooks should be avoided as the plague. Yesterday's best sellers which have not stood the test of time to become classics. The problem with these is millions were sold and everybody who would ever conceivably want to read them has already done so. I'm refering to titles such as *Love Story, Jaws, Hotel, Airport,* you get the idea. Titles which may be found in every flea market and Christian Thrift Store certainly don't belong on the shelves of a fine antiquarian book shop.

There are a number of subjects which are, for all practical purposes, unsaleable. I once donated over a thousand volumes on sociology after finally realizing the only ones I'd sold during an entire year were a few by Vance Packard. Political Science is just as dead. Economics is another section best never established. It requires eternal vigilance because these books are being constantly touted to you; they're like coat hangers. They must breed and multiply at night when the lights are out because, in spite of the fact I never take them in, they keep sprouting upon my shelves.

My weakness — one of many, actually — has always been old novels. You know the kind I mean. Pretty bindings with paper illustrations of lovely ladies on the front cover. Authors such as George Barr McCutcheon and a host of others from turn-of-the-century into the early thirties. Every store I ever had sported a nice big section of such stock. I never did sell enough out of it to justify even a fraction of the space but they were so charming I always expected to. So do like I say, not like I do. Hopefully you'll be stronger than I and not throw away perfectly good shelving on books nobody wants.

You'll want to have a Health section but 95 per cent of the material offered to you should be rejected. Nobody wants a twenty-five-year-old copy of *The Water Cure*. What sells are references such as current PDR's, *Merck Manual, Gray's Anatomy,* Medical and Nursing dictionaries, that sort of thing. Exercise books do well, especially aerobics and running. Beware of diet books; they tend to be like comets — very big splash very quickly but within a very short time no one wants them as a gift. Good nutritional books such as those published by Rodale Press are good stock.

Your business section is active but only if you steer clear of outdated material. There is no better way to waste your space than to stock five-year-old books on the stock market or outdated real estate material. With few exceptions you'd do well to stick to self-help type books. Anything from speed reading to memory improvement to the classic books of Carnegie and Peale make for solid sellers.

When it comes to paperbacks all of the above holds true plus the following. Gothics are dead; don't bother stocking them. I've seen the time you couldn't keep them on the shelf but that time is long gone.

General fiction pocket books with cover prices of less than $1.95 are likely to be losers unless you recognize the title or author as something special. Mind you, you mustn't attempt to apply this yardstick to other categories such as classics, mysteries or science fiction.

Biographies are avidly read by a substantial number of people but there seem to be an awful lot of very esoteric ones which nobody seems to want to read. If you recognize the name, chances are your clients will too. Presidents and their wives, theater personalities, writers, artists, these are a few of the better sellers. Business and union leaders, Victorian gentry, and scientists are among the poorer ones.

Books on World War I never sell for some reason. It's odd because books on the Civil War, WW II, Korea and Viet Nam sell very well. Strange, but I don't think I ever sold a book on WW I unless you count *Farewell To Arms*.

It's impossible to steel you against every possible pitfall, but the above should give you some idea of what to beware of. You'll soon see what's moving and what isn't. Listen to your customers; much of what I know about books I learned from my clients. Each collector is an expert within his own narrow little field of interest. Each knows far more about his subject than you probably ever will. And everybody loves a good listener.

The other thing you must learn to do is trust your instincts. Chances are they're pretty darn good if you'll just let them dictate when you're undecided. How can you go wrong? After all — you're the boss!

SMALL DETAILS CAN MAKE A BIG DIFFERENCE

The following little "tricks of the trade" I've gleaned from other successful booksellers or from personal experience and observation. Some are essential and others are merely sophisticated techniques which will increase sales.

This first one is absolutely essential. There is a popular philosophy in the antiquarian book industry that people want to be left alone in a shop and will resent any overtures which will be viewed as an attempt to sell them something. On the whole, I believe this philosophy is correct, but with one absolutely essential proviso. Every person who walks into your shop MUST be greeted in some way. It doesn't matter if it's a "Hi" or a "Good morning" or a "Howdy"; say SOMETHING!

There's a good reason for emphasizing this point so strongly, believe me. I've actually conducted a test once, instructing my staff not to say a word to incoming customers unless they spoke first. This is the usual custom in most shops. As I'd anticipated, over the two week period we conducted this test, dialogue between staff and customer decreased. Worse, so did sales. Think about it; doesn't it mean something positive to you when you walk into a store to have someone offer you a friendly greeting? Of course, if they proceed to swoop down on you and almost demand you buy something it quickly becomes a negative experience, but if you are just recognized with a pleasant welcome and left to your own devices it's a warm — and unique — experience these days.

But there's a lot more to it than just making your customer feel positive about his experience within your shop. I've found this simple device serves to make you accessible to your clients. Don't do it and here's what happens: people will stroll in, browse for a while, and stroll out without ever opening their mouths. The layout of your shop is somewhat complex to a first-time customer but unless you establish that simple relationship as they enter, most of them will never ask you for the assistance they need. During that two week period of the test I watched them. They would look longingly at the desk, sometimes approach it as if to ask for help, but most never did during the time we dispensed with the greeting. It's easy for your clients to find themselves overwhelmed in a shop which will have something in excess of fifty thousand books. They need your assistance in the beginning but unless you open the door verbally with that little word of acknowledgment, few will ask for it. It's such a simple thing but I'm convinced it represents the difference between success and failure for many a bookseller.

This next one may never make or break you but it will make some difference in your volume of sales. NEVER display duplicate copies of hardback books, particularly more expensive or collectable ones. The rationale seems to be that potential buyers seeing multiple copies will often feel they needn't pick it up then because it'll still be there later. That's an impression you never want to give. It diminishes the value and desirability of a book to show more than one copy. As soon as I realized that and began filing duplicates in the back room, the copies out front began to move more quickly.

Oddly enough, the above principle doesn't seem to hold true for paperbacks. Of course common sense dictates that if you have half a dozen copies of a title you're going to stop accepting it for a while, but having multiple copies of a GOOD paperback title on the shelf actually seems to promote sales. I think it's because paperbacks sort of blend into a sea of little titles on the shelf and multiple copies means those books stand out and get noticed and thus they sell.

I believe it was Ogden Nash who wrote "Nothing propinques like propinquity." He's right! At eighteen I was once the youngest advertising manager ever with Sears. One of the first things I learned was you could move anything if you could contrive to expose it to enough people. We would set up these big tables right inside the front door of the Sears store where I had my office; they were almost in the way, the customer had to sidle around them to get in or out of the store. On those tables went all the losers; the poorly-made shirts, the thin, homely towels, whatever. Things which had haunted their various departments for months, even years, sold out within days the moment they hit those tables. Of course they were discounted too, but the real secret was to expose them to every single person who walked in the door.

Same principle applies in your shop. You'll sell more books toward the front of the store than you will toward the rear. You'll sell more books from your window display than you will from the shelf. Use this fact. A book that's been lost on the shelf for a long time may have an attractive cover. If so, put it in the window or contrive somehow to display it face out. Never put plain books, especially fiction, on display in the window. Select those with vivid illustrations on the cover. If they don't sell within a couple of weeks, exchange them for something else. Once the honeymoon is over, get them out of there before your display goes stale.

Avoid the cluttered look so common in poorly-managed shops. Never file books horizontally — in stacks. Never jam so many books on a shelf that when someone tries to remove one book the ones on both sides want to come too. This destroys your books and encourages the client to return the book out of sequence where there might be more room. When you're filing books there's a tendency to want to make it fit and get rid of it but you must resist the urge to jam your shelves too full. It will rip your dust wrappers and spring your paperbacks if you do. Oh yes — another important principle! Most of your sales will be made from the middle-height range of shelves; books on topmost and bottom shelves will move much more slowly. Work within this factor by placing less active sections likely to attract more hardy, determined buyers at top and bottom. Sections such as archeology, hunting, fishing, auto repair, sports and true crime are naturals for the less accessible areas. Large sections covering more than one shelving unit must encompass top and bottom shelving, of course, but since the books are alphabetically arranged they'll pursue their authors high or low. But many casual customers are browsers and they seldom see anything below their knees or above their heads. It's another one of those fascinating facts you'll notice with amusement.

Keep your shop as immaculately clean as possible. You'll need a vacuum cleaner from time to time but pick up one of those Bissel carpet sweepers at

Sears and run it over your aisles each morning before opening. It's amazing how effective those little guys are. And invest a couple of dollars in a feather duster and make the rounds with it during the slow times. The best way to keep your store clean is to do a volume business so the books don't sit on the shelf too long. Change the filter on your heater and air conditioner every month.

Nothing does more to add charm and warmth to a shop than a few hanging plants up near the front. It's a minor nuisance to keep them watered and healthy but they say it's good for your soul.

I always like to hoke up my store with some fun things hanging from the ceiling. I've used Mother Goose mobiles and bushel baskets with stuffed animals peering over the side and flying witches on broomsticks. It gives things a festive air and brings a smile to faces of all ages. Your shop, after all, should be a fun place where people come to relax and enjoy themselves. You can help by setting the mood with a few such silly things.

Make it as easy as possible for people to find the subject sections they're interested in. The best way to do this is to label each section clearly. If you're feeling flush, Brodart offers a variety of engraved plastic signs to be mounted in each section. If not, a few sheets of poster board and a firm hand with a felt-tip marker will serve just as well. The other thing you can do is to find some two by three foot poster board at your friendly neighborhood office supply store and list every section to be found in each aisle. It's the same principle used by your local grocery store. Staple this big sign onto one of the cross braces you have running overhead in each aisle.

Keep a plastic bottle of Elmer's white glue handy for repairing cracked or shaken hinges. By standing the book up and opening both covers you can open the spine. Run a small bead of glue down along the hinge, waiting until it almost reaches the bottom. Then rest the book upon its spine and support it on either side by two heavy books. Within a few hours you should end up with a nice tight binding. Practice will make perfect; start on something cheap. Ultimately you will perform this repair upon good general stock, say anything over ten dollars. You should not attempt to do this to scarce collectable material however. Most collectors will resent any changes or repairs, preferring to have the book in its original state even with a cracked hinge.

10

Sales Made Outside the Store

They who can afford to give a second-hand bookseller what he asks in his catalogue, may in general do it with good reason, as well as a safe conscience. He is of an anxious and industrious class of men, compelled to begin the world with laying out ready money and living very closely; and if he prospers, the commodities and people he is conversant with generally end in procuring him a reputation for liberality as well as acuteness.

Leigh Hunt

QUOTING IS PROFITABLE IF IT'S DONE RIGHT

After your shop gets rolling I hope you'll take my earlier advice and subscribe to a weekly publication known as the *Antiquarian Bookman*. I've referred to it a number of times as the AB, which is how it is known throughout the industry. If you do subscribe you will receive a liberal education not only in current values but also what authors, titles and subjects are in demand. You'll quickly spot common denominators among the many published want lists in each week's issue. Certain illustrators, for example, are constantly being sought. Many dealers run permanent ads year after year for material in which they specialize. This information is money in the bank for you once you master the intricacies of "quoting."

At first you may be confused by the flurry of symbols, abbreviations and technical terms unique to the industry. It's easy for a neophyte to get lost in a blizzard of jargon like 24mo, TEG and elephant folio. In order, the foregoing terms mean: a book less than six inches in height, top edge gilt, and a large book twenty-four inches high or more. The key you'll need is either a copy of the Bookman's Glossary (See Chapter 19 for details.)

Any average well-run shop will acquire material which is being sought via want ads in the AB. If a dealer runs an ad, it tells you he has a buyer waiting for that book. But before you rush to offer him your copy there are some things you need to know.

I spelled out the five basic grades used to describe a book's condition in an earlier chapter. For purposes of quoting there are really only two grades: VG and F. (Very good and fine.) You may be able to sell a G (Good) copy of a reasonably scarce book in your shop, but almost never sight unseen through the mail. By the time you finished describing it honestly in your quote it would sound probably much worse than it is. In your shop a buyer might hold it in his hand and decide it wasn't all that bad. Learning to grade strictly is absolutely essential. One dealer I've bought a lot of books from always grades his books one grade lower than they actually are. He once explained to me, this way his clients were always pleasantly surprised when they received the book. It must work for I find myself dealing with him whenever possible.

As with all dealers, I've had to return books which were described as VG and turned out to be G at best. After this happens to you a time or two you find yourself passing over future offerings from that dealer. Conversely, you remember those dealers whose books always arrive as described; you tend to study their quotes and catalogues with extra care, hoping to find something to order.

Always submit quotes on three by five cards. If you don't, your quotes may not even be considered. Most active mail-order dealers are organized to require this sized quote in order to fit it into their files. If they are forced to recopy yours when it arrives they may well not bother. This would also be interpreted as the sign of an amateur and that wouldn't help your cause.

In the case of a single quote a post card is just the thing. For multiple quotes to the same dealer unlined file cards of the proper size are readily available or larger stock may be cut to size.

Always type your quotes if at all possible. Every time I run a want list I receive a surprising number of hand-written quotes which are quite indecipherable. We all find our own handwriting perfectly legible, but you must understand it might well prove otherwise to your intended reader. Again, it is a sign of professionalism and certainly a courtesy. After all, if you were to submit a holographic manuscript to a publisher it would certainly be returned unread.

So why do I keep getting all these quotes apparently written in cuneiform? Beats me! Not everyone has a typewriter at hand of course but there's a way around that. Hand printed quotes are entirely satisfactory. I tend to respond well to them because I perceive the quoter as being a careful and considerate individual.

Have a small hand stamp made up with your store name and address on it. It will come in handy as your return address stamp for the envelope but there's a more important use for it. Use it to stamp every quote you send out. Amazing as it might seem, lots of quoters will submit a handful of quotes on the proper-sized form but nowhere on the quotes does it say who or where they're from. Presumably there was a return address on the envelope they arrived in but that tends to be quickly discarded and the cards get sorted according to title, subject or author. Imagine your disappointment a week or two later — you've waited to see whether any better quotes come in — after you've checked with your customer and gotten the go-ahead to order, only to find you haven't a clue where the quote came from.

The above-mentioned delay is common practice among dealers. Many dealers and collectors receive their AB fourth class mail so dealers usually wait at least ten days from the time their ad hits to make their final decision. He may only want a single copy for a specific client; all other things being equal, he will naturally buy the least expensive copy.

Your quotes should be much more complete than those you see in the average ad in the AB. There's plenty of room to include extra details such as size, page count, illustrations if any, and anything else which is interesting or unique about the book. Always assume the buyer has never seen the book before. Detailed quotes result in sales. Remember, never more than one quote per card. In the paragraph above I said, all other things being equal, a dealer would buy the least expensive copy. All things will not be equal if you present a complete, professional quote and someone else sends him a sloppy, incomplete quote. He may well elect to pay the higher price rather than risk the necessity of returning the less expensive copy.

A quote should always state how long you are offering to reserve the book. Ten days to two weeks is standard. If you are not willing to hold it don't quote it. Nothing will alienate a dealer or collector more quickly than to respond with a check within a few days only to get the check back with a note telling them the book is no longer available.

You will soon develop a master list of collectors and dealers who have responded positively to your efforts. At the same time you will also develop a list of those who have never responded despite your best efforts. After about half a dozen quotes without result you'd be well advised to stop wasting your time with them. There are those in the business — usually part time dealers — who are unwilling to pay more than a small fraction of the value of any book; the sooner you weed them from your quote files the better.

As your quotes are returned to you with checks you will often find included permanent want lists from your satisfied customers. These lists are pure gold because you may rest assured you have a certain sale for any of the titles or authors on that list now and in the future. Permanent want lists from a dealer mean they are willing to buy in quantity, they are not just looking for a single copy. This is a sure sign of a real pro; it is a foolish dealer who spends money advertising in the AB for a scarce book, gets several quotes at fair prices, and buys only one. Permanent want lists reflect an ongoing special interest, so your future quotes will be very welcome indeed.

Once you have successfully completed a satisfactory transaction with someone, the next will be easier and more likely to occur. Any of us would opt to buy from someone we've dealt with before as opposed to a stranger if the choice is even close concerning quality and price. Before too long you'll find yourself in a position of complete mutual trust with certain dealers. You'll even be able to ship books with an invoice without even having to quote first in some cases. This high degree of mutual trust which exists within the bookselling community is one of the more satisfying and rewarding features of this extraordinary game.

The easiest way to knock off some quotes from the AB — or from the WANT LISTS you'll begin receiving after your first AB ad — is to scan through the "Books Wanted" section and make a check mark opposite each title or author you believe you have in stock. It will amaze you how you are able to retain the knowledge of just what is in stock. Then go back and pick up the ones you've checked and see whether or not your books on hand really do marry up to the wants. Are they the edition requested? Is their condition such that you may quote them as VG or better? Is it something which isn't likely to sell very quickly in your shop?

Make up a ''Quote Book'' showing what you quoted, to whom, and the price and date. Murphy's Law dictates that as soon as you quote a book and it's on hold, somebody's going to come along and just have to have that book. Merely refer to your Quote Book and let them know the date on which you'll be free to sell them the book in the event no check is forthcoming.

One more thing: if you don't want to sell a book, don't quote it. By that I mean you have to be willing to make it worth the buyer's while to order it. He's got to make a profit too, so there's no point in quoting it at full retail. As a general rule you should be discounting and quoting out material which isn't in great demand in your own shop.

Let me give you an example of what a proper quote should look like:

Milne, A.A. *The House At Pooh Corner,* Dutton 1928, 1st
U.S., F in F d.w., dec. Shepard, sm 8vo, 178 pgs.,
$100. pp & ins., ret. 10 days, hold 14 days.

There you have the author, title, publisher, date, the fact that it is a first United States edition (first British is worth much more because Milne is British and book was published there first), condition of book and dust wrapper are stated as fine, decorations are by Shepard, it is slightly smaller than the average book, page count is 178, price, you are including postage and insurance, buyer has the right of return within ten days of receiving it and you are promising to hold it for two weeks from the date of your quote pending his decision.

PREPARING A PROPER AD

After you've been in business for six months or so, with any luck at all you should be in a position to field a nice ad of your own in the AB. There are a number of reasons for doing this, not the least of which is a pretty good chunk of money for your coffers. Perhaps even more importantly, it will begin to establish you in the eyes of your peers as an important shop. A professionally-done ad will generate a steady stream of catalogues and want lists which translate into ever increasing opportunities to buy and sell better books. It will also appraise buyers and collectors of your existence so that they might add you to their itinerary when they head out on their next buying trip.

A full-page ad in the AB requires one hundred and thirty-eight lines. Each line is a half column consisting of thirty-eight spaces. I've always believed a full-page ad gets more attention than does a partial page back in the classified section. It takes an average of about sixty books to justify a full page ad. They should all be VG or better, quite desirable for whatever reason, and certainly in the price range of twenty-five dollars and up. Preferably up.

If you study the AB you'll notice there are always some ads which leave you with a lot of unanswered questions. The ones which especially irritate are those which state, ''All books are VG or better,'' in the heading of the ad and then go on to merely list their books. Very often — in fact, usually — a collector will accept only fine so this leaves you hanging. You may only assume the worst: that any book you need from the list is VG only. Unless the dealer is offering his books for far below market, such an ad is a mistake. Never do it! Give a fair grading of both book and wrapper for each and every book in your ad.

Another variation of the above error is the dealer who describes his books as ''F in d.w.'' Does he mean the wrapper is fine too? Who knows? Another minor irritant is the dealer who doesn't include postage in the price of the book. I received a catalogue recently from a bookseller who wasted half of the first page lamenting the fact that fully half of his orders arrived with the postage incorrectly computed, forcing him to write back giving the revised figures. Little wonder! This fellow had evolved a complicated system of so much postage for the first book, a lower per book cost up to a certain number of books, then yet another figure when another level of volume was attained. I'm not at all surprised; the wonder of it is half of his buyers got it right. This guy must have been a former IRS agent. In an obvious attempt to encourage larger orders he obfuscated himself to the point of silliness. His entire problem could be solved completely by simply pricing his books post paid. I'll wager I'm not the only dealer who threw up his hands in disgust and went on to the next catalogue.—Some dealers do this in a foolish attempt to make the price of their books appear as low as possible. In reality, all they do is needlessly complicate their transactions. Most of us may not be mathematical wizards but I think we can add or subtract the cost of shipping when weighing the cost of a book. (It really shouldn't even be a factor; shipping books, even going foreign, is the biggest bargain around.)

There are plenty of well-written ads in the AB in any given issue which may be used as models. Here is the way you would advertise the same Milne book in the AB:

Milne, A.A. *House At Pooh Corner,* Dutton 1928,
1st U.S., F in F d.w. $100.

The first few lines of your ad — the heading — should provide the following information: phone number and store hours so clients will know when they may phone in orders. If postage and insurance is included and, if not, how much to add to the price of each book ordered. CWO means cash with order; if you don't spell this out some dealers may expect you to ship and bill. Shipping and billing is fine later on and regular clients have the right to expect it. Library orders are always ship and bill; you may wait several months to get paid at times but they always come through.

The final thing you need in you heading is your policy on accepting returns. It's universally understood within the industry that all mail-ordered books are returnable. It could scarcely be otherwise: your clients must buy sight unseen. Still, always state it. It reassures the faint of heart. It's an encouraging and positive statement which reinforces the image that your offering is a good one and you are proud of it. Of course, nothing you might put in this introduction will help if your books are not as described so remember to be on the conservative side in your grading.

Now don't panic when you do get a book returned. I can assure you there isn't a dealer in the business who doesn't. Show me a man who claims he doesn't and I'll show you a fibber. No matter how careful you are, you'll always get a few back. I'd guess the irreducible minimum on returns is something on the order of 3 per cent. Some occur simply due to buyer's remorse, the same spectre which haunts all retailers. Or a dealer orders a book for a client and by the time it arrives the client suffers a change of heart. Some dealers will then return the book. It is foolish and unfair, but they'll do it. When this happens to me I always keep the book, no matter how esoteric it might be. If it's a scarce book in the condition stated I'm pleased to have it in stock. Besides which I wouldn't have the gall to return it when the seller committed no error. By ordering it you removed it from the market and probably deprived the seller of other opportunities to move it so I would never return any book unless there's been some fudging on the grading. And that is certainly a somewhat sub-jective thing. There's ample room for debate between fair men on the sub-ject. In the end it is the buyer alone who must be satisfied and his decision honored.

In order to avoid suffering any loss from returns when running your ads, always take at least one back-up order for each book offered. That way if you should get it back all you'll have to do is send it on to the back-up buyer along with an invoice. Explain to the back-up buyer that the book is already on hold but that you like to have a second client just in case the first doesn't follow through with a check. (This happens rarely but it happens.) Tell him if you haven't received a check from the first buyer within a week you will ship and bill. He will be grateful for the consideration even though he probably won't get the book.

PREPARING A PROPER WANT AD

There is another highly profitable type of ad you will want to run in the AB and that is the "Want Ad." These are the ads you see in the front of the AB which normally take up at least 80 per cent of the periodical. This alone should tell you something. Shortly after you open for business you will begin to receive requests from your customers for out-of-print books. Some will be common enough so that all you need do is file their request until a copy comes in. Obtain their name and daytime phone number on a three by five file card. Leave all new cards out in some designated place until all staff has had a chance to see them. Amazingly enough, a bell will usually go off in the baby midbrain of whoever takes the title in and the client will be called. This file should also be worked during slow times by new employees. A surprising number of sales result when this is done. Even though some of the calls may be concerning inappropriate material or the client has already acquired the book wanted, the calls are extremely productive. Your customers never fail to be pleased and impressed to find you really are working to fill their needs. When they begin to talk you up within the community as "their bookseller" — the same way people talk up "their" doctor, lawyer and stock broker — you'll know you've arrived.

Others will be more scarce and these will be the material for your first Want Ad. As in the case of a Books For Sale ad, I firmly believe better results are to be obtained by waiting until you can muster a full-page ad rather than just a few lines in the back classified section of the AB. (Also, the per-line rate is less for a full-page ad.) It takes a good many wants to make up an ad; each book seldom requires more than one line, so that means one hundred and thirty eight books. Actually, in some cases you won't even be specifying titles but merely authors. For instance, regional authors who are of special interest in your area because they write about local history will be in heavy demand. Thus you will have in your ad: "Anything by..."

You needn't wait until you have firm "wants" for one hundred and thirty eight books to run a Books Wanted ad. It's the best way I know to fill up your "hot" sections, the ones which cannot be maintained as well as you'd like through over-the-counter trades and purchases. Such sections might be Art, Illustrated or LEC's (Limited Edition Club). Fill out your ad by requesting those types of books experience has taught you will sell readily if offered in your shop.

The response from a well-written Books Wanted ad can be very exciting. I've received many of the finest books I've ever had the thrill of owning through these ads. It's like the best Christmas you ever imagined when the quotes begin arriving. And it just goes on; I've gotten quotes as long as four months after an ad ran.

When you think you're ready to make up an ad, call those clients from whom you've taken "wants" and ask them to stop in your shop. It's time to qualify your people. I think it's a good idea to charge them a "search" fee at some point. Not so much for the money as to qualify their sincerity. Some fill out "wants" on the spur of the moment and later on may not be willing to pay the price of a scarce book. Others may have already obtained a copy somehow. The only way I know to weed out the faint-hearted is charge a "search" fee. The added bonus is that you've already made a handsome profit on the ad before it's even published. Most shops seem to charge about five dollars for one request, with perhaps a somewhat reduced rate for additional titles from the same client. Frankly, I think that's a bit steep, but I must agree with the consensus within the industry that it is essential to require proof of your customers' sincerity. But I do think about three dollars would serve the purpose as well, as long as ad rates hold steady.

One more thing: don't make the foolish mistake so many dealers are guilty of and buy only one copy of scarce and desirable titles when they are offered. You may not want to display more than one copy at a time — I urge you not to — but it may be difficult or even impossible to replace one copy when it's gone so use your head. If price and condition are right on subsequent quotes, order several — if it's fine material it's money in the bank. Nothing frustrates me more than the dealer who goes to the time and expense of running an AB ad requesting some really "special" book, gets two or three equally fine quotes for it but buys only one. The moment he sells it he's right back where he started.

PROPER SHIPPING OF BOOKS

Once you begin making sales outside the store it's time to give some serious thought to making certain the books arrive intact, just as fine as they left your hands. This vital area of the business deserves some consideration; it is another way in which your peers will make a snap judgment of your professionalism. Your mastery of it will influence your far-flung clientele greatly, either pro or con. I certainly form an opinion the moment I unwrap a box of books from another dealer. I don't think I'll ever forget — or forgive — the man who shipped me fourteen first edition OZ books by the simple expedient of merely tossing them loose into a box. Thousands of dollars worth of books and he packed them as if their total value was something under five dollars. There are other less blatant, and less obvious, errors to be avoided so commit the following to heart and memory.

For shipping one or two books I like the Book Mailing Bags available from Brodart. (Address under Reference to Suppliers.) These well-padded "jiffy bags" are already stamped for book-rate shipping. They are easy to either staple or tape closed. The size which is most suitable is the 10½" x 16" but you'll find you'll also need some of the 12½" x 19" for oversized books. But you mustn't think you can just drop a book into the mailer, seal it and send it.

First check the book carefully, erasing all traces of pricing, then wrap it in several layers of paper. Never use newspaper for the inner wrapping of a book. Printer's ink, by its very nature, doesn't dry completely for a very long time and is therefore likely to smudge or stain the cover or dust wrapper. Get in the habit of saving all kinds of paper in addition to newspaper. Rolls of plain brown wrapping paper may be obtained very inexpensively. Use masking tape to secure the paper; it adheres well and is cheap. After a suitable inner wrap, a double thickness of newspaper will provide additional protection.

You're still not finished. Now cut an oblong piece of cardboard from a box, sized to fit somewhat loosely into the mailer. Trim the corners round. Left squared, the corners will tend to damage the mailer as it's tossed about en route. Now you're ready to seal it up, right? Wrong! Never ship without placing the name and address of the sendee inside. That way if the package should become damaged the Post Office can repack it and send it on. Believe it or not, they'll do it, too.

In case you're still wondering what the oblong piece of cardboard was for, that's to prevent the book itself from having to absorb the slings and arrows of outrageous handling. This way the cardboard stiffener arrives with the bumped corners instead of the book.

Address and return should be printed on the outside wrapper directly using a felt-tipped marking pen. Labels tend to fall off or be removed by postal handling machines.

Now you've got it ready to go—what to do with it? The cost of shipping UPS or book rate via the the Post Office is pretty much the same. Fortunately for us, Ben Franklin was a bookseller before becoming the first Postmaster General and organizing the Post Office. That's why there's a special rate for books which is surprisingly inexpensive. In the end you'll undoubtedly decide between the two on the basis of convenience but if both are handy I'd advise you to go with UPS. UPS will get it there a little more quickly and there may not be quite as intense an effort to destroy the book. You also save a bit on books valued at under one hundred dollars because insurance to that amount is automatically included with UPS. You have to pay for all insurance with the Postal Service. By the way, you may as well be advised that the Post Office does not pay claims based upon the amount of insurance. Yes, you read it right! It doesn't mean a damn to them what you insured it for in the event of a claim; all that matters is what THEY deem a fair reimbursement. It's a sweet little scam they've had going for decades. People naively assume they are insuring their packages in the amount of the insurance they purchase on it. HAH! I'm here to tell you it ain't so.

Insurance over and above one hundred dollars with UPS is also extra. One of the things I like about them is the higher limit on insurance. You can't obtain more than four hundred dollars coverage with the Postal Service. UPS likes to limit theirs to one thousand but that's usually enough if you take it into account when you package. Anything over the thousand dollar limit would have to be sent via one of the private couriers such as Purolater.

When it comes to insurance, don't be penny-wise and pound foolish and neglect to buy it. It's really a bargain at the price. Most dealers believe in self-insuring up to a certain point — say fifty dollars. It's your decision but bear in mind you must face the very real possibility of eating the loss yourself whenever you ship without it. Actually, the prospect isn't too terrible. I've lost a total of, I believe, fifteen books over the years. Considering the fact that most of those were in a single box and taking into account the many thousands of books I've shipped, it's not too shabby at all.

Now let's deal with those orders involving more than one or two books. You'll need to keep a supply of small to medium boxes ready. As above, each book will still have to be individually wrapped. Never place the books in direct contact with any of the surfaces of the box — bottom, sides or top. If you've ever seen the way they throw them around you'll understand. Wadded newspapers are fine for a buffer; the packing material I call plastic peanuts is better and costs very little. Whatever the material, you must end up with the books resting against a cushion of it on all six sides.

As with the "jiffy bag," make sure you place the name and address of the buyer inside on top before closing.

The question of what kind of tape to use can get involved. There are a surprising number of poor products being marketed. I once purchased a large roll of so-called package tape at a Post Office. It was fascinating stuff: it self-destructed at the slightest touch when wet and wouldn't stick to cardboard. For price and quality I've settled on a plastic tape marketed by Brodart. It is their Sealing Tape 32 491 001 and comes in 60 yard rolls two inches in width.

Begin with a strip at right angles to your flaps to hold them in closed position, lapping it down the sides a few inches. Then run tape right over the seam, again lapping well over at both ends. I also like to run tape along both ends to seal the sides of the top flaps. Common sense is the key: the heavier the weight of the box the more precaution is required. You would do well to keep the size and weight of any one box to a reasonable minimum.

If there is enough clear space on the top of the box to permit the address and return to be done with trusty felt-tipped pen, do so. If the box is making its third or fourth trip and there's just no room remaining, settle for an address label. But never trust the label alone; they're too easily damaged or dislodged. Keep a special roll of two inch wide clear Scotch tape just for the purpose of covering over labels. Two strips cover it completely and now you may trust it.

And don't forget you have to clearly label the box "books" in order to get the special book rate at the Post Office. This isn't necessary if you are shipping UPS.

Make it a hard and fast rule to ship within forty-eight hours of receiving an order. There's no better way to endear yourself to your clients. I've run into one or two dealers who won't ship until the buyer's check has cleared. That tells me more about those dealers than it does their clientele. I'm very pleased to be able to say I've NEVER gotten a bum check from either a dealer or a collector so why insult your best friends?

BENEFITS OF COOPERATING WITH NEW BOOK STORES

You're missing a great deal if you don't establish a warm working relationship with as many of the new book stores in your area as possible. It's the ideal marriage: both parties come out better off than they were before. Your contribution is to get on the phone whenever one of your customers wants an in-print book. Call a new book store which is willing to reciprocate, find out whether they have the title, and if not whether they are willing and able to order it. Don't just send the customer over there — CALL THEM! That way you're reminding them every time you are there and you are helping them be successful. The implication that you expect and deserve the same consideration will not be lost on them. Of course it works far better with the independently-owned stores where you're dealing directly with the owner than it does with the chain operations but even the chains are very competitive and usually managed by bright and caring people who respond well to this reasonable approach.

The other side of the coin is that the new store owner runs into customers all the time who want out-of-print titles. The average reader has no way of knowing what's in or out of print, after all. If you're fulfilling your end of the bargain, there's no reason in the world why they won't gladly refer these clients to you. There isn't one damn thing a new store owner can do to help them other than that. I know one enterprising antiquarian dealer who's had cards printed requesting a search service for out-of-print titles. He provides the cards to new store owners, allowing them to retain the cash for each card filled out. That way the new store earns some extra income, the used dealer picks up a client free and the customer's needs are served. What could be better?

SHOULD YOU PUBLISH A CATALOGUE?

There's only one answer—it depends! Several years into the business, after your list of special clients has grown to at least several hundred, it's a decision you'll have to make. Two main factors will dictate your decision: how specialized have you become and what is the cost of producing your list?

As to the former, the more specialized you have become the more targeted and therefore cost efficient a catalogue would be. If, for example, you come to deal heavily in Western Americana and have built a list of several hundred dealers, collectors and libraries appropriate to that subject, by all means begin publishing catalogues for direct mailing. By this time you will have received plenty of catalogues from other dealers so you may select a format you like and one which you can afford. These range all the way from handsome slick illustrated catalogues to barely legible mimeographed lists. The value of your offering will determine a reasonable budget for your own mailing. Many dealers manage to make arrangements with friends who have access to photocopiers. Thus they are able to run off their own lists during off hours, often for nothing more than the cost of the paper.

If, on the other hand, your interests are as varied as are mine and most store owners, you'll get far better results from a well-constructed AB ad. Such an ad reaches over ten thousand dealers, collectors and library purchasing agents world wide. Many are passed on to more than one potential customer. I've sold quite a few books to clients who wrote they were given my ad by their bookseller. The vast majority of these people—the crème de la crème of buyers at any given time—are not on my mailing list and there is no other way I know of reaching them. I can offer an average of sixty-five books, described in full detail, per page. Say I take out a four-page ad; total cost to me is three hundred and twenty dollars. I can thereby expose nearly three hundred books to something in excess of ten thousand potential buyers, most of whom are unknown to me. Even if I somehow contrived to get my catalogue printed free I couldn't begin to pay the postage on more than about 15 per cent of those clients for the same money, even if I did know where to send them.

Also bear in mind there's no way you can add any new clients by a catalogue mailing. There are lots of dealers who seldom or never run AB ads and who swear by putting out lists direct to their clients on a pretty regular basis. One of their arguments is that an AB ad is history a week after it comes out, replaced by the next issue. A catalogue may be kept around and studied at leisure. Sounds good, but my experience tells me catalogues, like AB ads, are scanned very quickly the instant they come to hand and decisions to buy or not to buy are made on the spot. They have to be because if it looks good to you it surely will look good to others as well. So much for the leisure of a catalogue.

I think the truth of the matter is store owners dealing in general stock and all subjects are just too busy and too successful to fool with catalogues. They are more appropriate to highly specialized dealers, particularly mail-order dealers without a retail store. It's something to look forward to in your twilight years: sitting in front of your computer punching out catalogues. I'm quite serious; keep an accurate list of all your buyers for that very purpose. It's money in the bank toward your retirement years. What better way to spend your "golden years" than traveling part of the year buying stock and sitting home the rest of the time sending out catalogues between soaps on TV? Okay, so I was kidding about the soaps, but the rest I'm dead serious about. Think about it; it's got to be the greatest gambit ever. Personally, I'm planning a book-buying trip to Germany and France next summer.

11

Hiring Help
That
Won't Hurt

What are my books?—My friends, my loves,
My church, my tavern, and my only wealth;
My garden: yea, my flowers, my bees, my doves:
My only doctors—and my only health.

                                    Richard Le Gallienne

WHAT TO LOOK FOR IN AN ASSISTANT

The major problem with hiring someone in this business is selecting from the plentitude of applicants. This is a romance business to book lovers of all ages. The only problem is many of them visualize themselves sitting around all day enjoying all those lovely books. One Saturday afternoon in the store would send them screaming off to the nearest unemployment office.

Many's the offer I've had from those who were willing to work for no money at all — just books! Reject such offers out of hand — it could easily cost you a fortune. No, not in books. In lost sales. There'll be many an offer to work for minimum wage from retired teachers and librarians all the way to book-crazed teenagers. Your desirable employee isn't to be found within this group either but if all you need is a part-time clerk to shelve books and stand behind the counter to make change, fine. Any of the above might do.

But what we're concerned with here is an alter ego for you. Someone who can take over fully and completely while you take trips or just stay home and play vegetable when you need to. Probably by the time you're ready to hire someone full-time you'll have a handle on the demands of the business. By then you'll know physical stamina is high on the list of qualifications. When your shop is successful enough to warrant an assistant you'll be taking in and putting out between five hundred and a thousand books a day, every day. Each and every one must be filed in the right order and in the right section. Boxes of books are heavy, which makes that dear little retired librarian an unlikely choice. Of the employees I've had over the years, the very best all shared certain common denominators. First of all they've been exactly divided between men and women so there's no criteria there. A woman well into her middle years has adequate strength and as for stamina she'll work a guy into the ground more often than not. Come to think about it, a disproportionate number of the shops I admire most are owned and/or operated by women.

There's no nice way to put it: the perfect employee is a hyperactive sociopath. I once hired one and he was beautiful. As long as there was a warm body in the store he'd be merrily hyping away, (and in the process selling one hell of a lot of books). When the store was empty he'd rush around straightening shelves and dusting — a real three month wonder! Therein lies the flaw; sociopaths aren't any good over the long haul. So you've got to look for someone a bit nearer the norm but with a liberal dose of the sociopathic traits. (It's illegal to give them speed so you have to find someone who was born with an edge on.)

A profile of the ideal assistant would go something like this. He or she would enjoy a high level of energy, be an avid reader and project a pleasant demeanor. It's not much to ask, really. He doesn't have to be a Rhodes Scholar by any means but he will have to be able to make all those myriad little judgments quickly, as you've been doing. Look for signs of self-assurance, someone who's happy in their own skin. It would help if they could tell the difference between a classic and a potboiler. Take nothing for granted. I once hired a guy with a Master's in English Lit. who didn't know the difference between Joseph Conrad and Sidney Sheldon. I couldn't believe it. Finally I made up a list of twelve names, six of them major classic writers. The only one he recognized was Dickens.

Priority number one is certainly to avoid anyone you believe might suffer from chronic ambivalence. It could well be terminal in this business and there's an awful lot of it going around. The whole idea, after all, is for you to be set free as soon as they're trained. No day will go by, hopefully, when there won't be literally hundreds of decisions to be made. Not one of them is likely to be of any major consequence but most people just don't have any talent for it. The world is chock full of those who can work full tilt all day long and do a bang-up job just as long as someone else remains at the helm. Start presenting them with options and they're agonizing over each and every one. It's true! I once met a girl who had recently left her husband. When I asked why, she said it was because he couldn't decide where to park. Apparently he'd drive around the block two or three times if there were more than one parking spot, unable to decide between them. Now that's ambivalence.

Fortunately there are others who thrive on it and that's the main thing I'd advise you to look for. Devise some simple little test once you think you've got a serious candidate. Give him a stack of books to be divided up into takers and rejects. After supplying some brief guidelines, stand back. It doesn't matter in the least how he segregates the books, mind you. What you'll be watching for is to observe how comfortable he is with the simple process of making decisions. If he does it swiftly without grimacing and ends up with a "what the hell!" shrug, hire him.

I'll pass along a great way to learn one hell of a lot about someone in a hurry just in case you can ever arrange it. When you think you've got a winner, conjure up some excuse to get them to drive you somewhere. It needn't be far. I can tell you more about someone's personality after riding with them a mile in traffic than I could after sitting in a room talking to them for a week. Do they operate their vehicle as an extension of themselves, flowing smoothly with the traffic and, seemingly without conscious thought, take advantage of openings as they occur but never at any cost to other drivers? Or is their car a foreign object in their hands, erratically hurrying from silly jackrabbit start to sudden stop? Do they wear the harried frown of the chronically poor driver? Think about it next time you're riding with someone; see whether their driving doesn't reflect their TRUE personality as clearly as any day-long psychological profile test would.

SALARY STANDARDS WITHIN THE INDUSTRY

Lousy! That, in a word, describes salary standards within the industry. You may be certain it also explains why most poorly-run shops don't begin to do the volume of business they could and should enjoy.

All too often it is the custom for shop owners to pay clerks minimum wage. Because there will always be a multitude of applicants for the job they figure why pay more? If only I could convince them their niggardly policy may well be costing them tens of thousands annually. But I've tried a time or two to no avail. The problem is, such negative thinking is merely symptomatic of an overall philosophy which probably permeates every facet of their conduct of business, relegating it all to its lowest mean rather than its highest.

Please don't make that mistake. Even if you got lucky and landed the kind of assistant we talked about above, how long do you think you could hang on to him? All you'll end up doing is endlessly training a succession of losers or people who will always keep looking for something better.

There's a better way to do it. Read on and I'll explain just how it works.

WHY YOU SHOULD NEVER PAY A STRAIGHT HOURLY WAGE

You never pay someone a straight hourly wage for the same reason you never enter them in a race and then chain them to the starting gate. The idea is to unfetter them and allow them to attain their highest potential, not limit them to the lowest level of performance their conscience allows. No salesman worth a damn I ever heard of worked for straight hourly wages. Mark Twain once said there was only one real job in the world — sales. That may be debatable but sales is certainly the job of your employees. If you want performance you'd better get used to the idea of structuring your pay scale to make it happen.

As a very young man I once wasted some years of my working life with a small pharmaceutical company. Sales staff were paid straight salary with the meager exception of an annual bonus. Management was forever bemoaning the fact that turnover was so great. Many of us in sales kept hammering away at the idea of putting us on commission but management was reluctant. They used the lame excuse that accountability was a problem in spite of the fact that most or all of the more successful drug houses were already paying their field men via commission. And of course the weaker individuals with the company were dead set against it as well.

It was a crying shame because the company had a really excellent training program and spent a small fortune making their men productive. We were so well-trained that one of the really big pharmaceutical companies paid their salesmen a handsome bonus if they could recruit one of us. There were quite a few bonuses paid.

The net result of this foolhardy attitude was that the company served the industry as a training ground, yet seldom reaped any of the benefits of its own efforts. The best of the salespeople soon realized their own self-worth and went where the rewards were commensurate with their skills. The weak people hung on forever because the straight salary was a haven for them; commission may well have spelled a cut in pay for many of them. But worst of all, I believe, was the attitude this policy caused those of us in the field to hold toward the company. It caused us to feel like fools if we worked too hard. I think each of us tried in his own way to calculate what constituted a fair return of effort for the money paid. Of course we all calculated that differently. One of the company's top salesmen put himself through law school, attending full time while the company thought he was out there making calls. The point is few of us were willing to go that extra mile, make that extra call which would have meant so very much to the company cumulatively.

That's how not to do it. But I'm glad I had the experience of observing that corporate error because it's made me a lot of money since. I have NEVER hired anyone full-time — not after the first thirty days — on straight wage. And I don't mean just sales people in my shops; I'm talking about every employee in every business I've ever been involved in. It's a fair list. After I got into the antiquarian book business and the profits began rolling in I found myself in the position of having to do things with the money. Among other things I've owned three hotels, a warehouse, rental property ranging from duplexes to eight units, laundromats and farms.

Basically what I do is very simple. I set aside 5 per cent of the increase in the GROSS over last year's figures for the same month and pay it out in commissions. Always pay commissions based upon the gross because it's too easy to play games with the net. Any intelligent employee knows this so it wouldn't be fair, nor would it have the desired impact to profitshare based on the net.

Now think about it for a minute. You're giving away 5 per cent of the INCREASE in the gross over year-ago figures. You're pocketing 95 per cent. Given the profit margins we're working with in the used book business it's the deal of the century.

Believe me — it works! When I bought my first hotel and explained the plan to the staff the transformation was almost unbelievable. Instead of merely occupying space behind the desk my desk men began calling around to the other hotels and motels in the area and letting them know we still had vacancies. As soon as the others filled up they began referring customers to us. The maids began showing up on a regular basis, something which was uncommon in the past. The first antiquarian book store I ever owned I bought as a going concern. Along with it I inherited a full-time clerk and that's all she was — a clerk. I put her on the 5 per cent program from day one and, lo and behold, she turned into a tiger! Instead of just putting in her time she began to SELL! She started calling me up at home when she was on to brag about the big sale she'd just made. She stopped reading books behind the counter and began working the customers. As the end of the month drew near she took an active interest in how the numbers were shaping up and comparing them to the last year's sales for the month. In short, she became INVOLVED. She became as deeply interested and determined as I was to make those numbers grow. (They did; that's why I had to buy all those hotels.)

Within a matter of a few months volume in that first store doubled. This made for some very handsome commission checks for her. They couldn't be big enough to suit me. Remember, I got to keep 95 per cent of the increase. As it worked out, paying my employee 5 per cent of the gross was tantamount to paying her 10 per cent of the net increase. It was a grand bargain for both of us and you never saw two more pleased people in your life. And you never saw more of a change come over someone in their working persona. I practically had to throw cold water over her at times. Her enthusiasm was contagious of course and in turn hyped the store and lead to even greater sales.

In the past it was her custom to announce the imminent closing of the shop as the hour drew near. Now she just grinned at late-arriving customers and gladly stayed until the last possible sale was made. She now had a vested interest; it was HER store, too.

It's that simple. Pay a base salary of minimum wage or just a little over but pay the commission. Never pass up an opportunity to pay out a dollar and get back ten. And as for turnover, the only way you'll ever have any is if your manager gets hit by a Mack truck.

Note I said MANAGER. Even though you may only have one employee, assign him the title, manager. It may sound like a small thing to you but, especially if he's young, it will likely mean quite a lot to him. It may make a difference when he's filling out credit applications, for instance. It will certainly make a difference in his attitude towards you. It's impossible to stress the importance of this relationship too much. After you're successful and established you are not going to want to be married to your shop seven days a week. You'll want to be free to travel and not have to worry about the shop. This means your manager will have to be empowered to write checks, make deposits, all the things you do when you're there. The more you can do to maintain this feeling of proprietorship on the part of your employees the better your chances of achieving this.

Don't neglect to provide your help with medical insurance also. The increase in the premium over and above what it would cost you and your family is minimal. As a small businessman you will find you are eligible for quite a variety of insurance plans at surprisingly reasonable rates. As a matter of fact, many of the plans require a minimum of three insured parties in order to eliminate husbands and wives who form pseudo-businesses just to become eligible for inexpensive insurance coverage.

To put it simply: treat your employees as you would that goose who lays the fourteen karat eggs. If you do it right and are just a little bit lucky, that's exactly what they'll be. Now let me tell you what is likely to happen on payday. Most of the store employees I ever had couldn't wait to receive their checks so they could endorse them back over to me and take out the value in books. I had one young man who was my only employee at the time and he was making quite a lot of money due to the bonus plan. I also make it a policy to offer all employees 50 per cent off on general stock books and 25 per cent on collectables. Every payday this guy would have a stack of first editions set aside; he never took a check out of the store. His wife, who was a nurse, began coming in on paydays, hanging around and giving both of us dirty looks. I felt guilty but there was no dissuading this guy. He worked for me a long time, until I sold the store, and he liked to pick my brain concerning the book business. I guess it all came out all right though; the last I heard he was running his own book shop in Oakland.

He may have been the extreme example but every single one of my employees ended up taking out some portion of their wages in books. It's almost a matter of the more you pay them, the less you pay them.

12

Treating Your Special Books in Special Ways

There is nothing like books, of all things sold incomparably the cheapest, of all pleasures the least palling; they take up little room, keep quiet when not wanted, and when taken up, bring us face to face with the choicest men who have ever lived, at their choicest moments.

Samuel Palmer

NOTE ON THE HISTORY AND IMPORTANCE OF BOOKS

In 1986 the Government of the United States proposed beginning construction of a Library of Congress Book Deacidification* facility. It is to be built near Frederick, Maryland, on the grounds of the U.S. Army Base, Fort Detrick. Estimated cost of the plant is pegged at eleven and one-half million dollars. It is hoped the plant will have the capacity of treating as many as one million books per year.

The process changes paper from acidic to slightly alkaline, which effectively increases the life expectancy of the books four or five times over. Operating cost is estimated to be two and one-half million dollars annually. The facility will employee twenty-two persons per shift and is slated to operate twenty-four hours a day, seven days per week.

I find the above fact fascinating in view of the prognosticators who are fond of stating there is no longer any valid reason for books. Information may be more efficiently stored and retrieved on micro-chips, the popular

Editor's note:
*As of this printing this facility had not yet been completed.

wisdom goes. Apparently the government doesn't agree. They remind me a lot of the pundits of the last century who opined there was no further need of paintings, now that the camera had come into being.

On October 16th, 1984, the Post Office issued a twenty-cent commemorative stamp entitled "A Nation of Readers." The stamp features a likeness of Abraham Lincoln reading to his son, Todd. Its introduction highlights the importance to this nation of books and reading.

For those of you who are archivists, the earliest known books were written in Korea, in the Chinese language, somewhere around 750 A.D. The famous Bibles of Gutenberg were first seen in 1455. What is not so commonly known is that seventy-eight years earlier the Koreans were using movable print to turn out books featuring the teachings of Buddha.

CREATIVE DISPLAY ENHANCES YOUR CHANCES

Should you elect to work your way up into finer and finer stock, and I sincerely hope you will, you soon arrive at a point where you can no longer merely shove all your books onto open shelves. That is, unless you don't mind precocious five-year-olds grabbing your five hundred dollar leather-bounds and practicing their frisbee techniques. Nothing displays this sort of material to better advantage than the style of case usually known as a lawyer's bookcase. This is commonly a four-tiered case, sometimes stackable and sometimes not, with glass fronts which open out and up, the front then sliding back into the case. The authentic old ones have all manner of trick hinges and pulleys. Fortunately there are plenty of modern replicas around which serve nearly as well.

It is the custom among many dealers to keep these cases locked, forcing a would-be client to request that it be opened so he may have a look at the books. That is a major mistake. You are not in business to offend people. Presumably you are in business to make money. Locking these cases accomplishes the former beautifully and prevents the latter almost as well.

The first shop I bought had several such cases — all locked. After several weeks it came to me that no one had ever requested they be opened and the sight of the padlocks had a very disquieting effect on me. Finally I decided to try an experiment, so I opened all of them and put away the locks. A few days later a lady entered the shop, walked over to the cases, lifted one of the front hatches and began removing books. She took a long time examining them, bearing little stacks over to the counter from time to time, then going back to continue working her way through all the shelves. She ended up spending well over a thousand dollars that day, by far the largest single sale I'd ever enjoyed at the time. As I was totaling the sale she told me she'd wanted the books for a very long time but was so insulted by the locked cases she'd never have bought them if I hadn't discarded the locks. She told me, along with others, that there was almost no turnover within those cases, that the same books had been there for years. As soon as I threw away the fetters my only problem was finding better stock to keep those cases full.

The moral is evident: avoid all negatives in your shop. Locked cases are negatives. So are signs which threaten or demean. For instance, I'd never put up a sign which read, "No Smoking." I never allow smoking in my stores, understand, but that's too cold. Instead I put up a sign which says, "Our Bodies And Our Books Thank You For Not Smoking." Now I've gotten the same message across but in a positive way which comes across as grateful instead of insulting. These little things are cumulatively very important. A big food chain may be able to get away with insult signs such as "Shoplifters Will Be Prosecuted" or "Ten Dollar Charge For Returned Checks" but you can't. And why would you want to? Only a curmudgeon would even want to put up such nasty messages for his clients to read. If that sort of thing appeals to you, go back to the book store and see if you can't trade this in on a copy of *Do It To Him Before He Does It To You.*

Back to those cases: the fact that they are closed is enough to stop the idle curious from handling your expensive tomes. Another way you may protect your delicate and costly books is to simply shelve them behind you at the checkout counter. They make an impressive background for your smiling face and it's a display no one can miss while they're paying for their books. Even for those customers who'll never buy anything more than paperbacks, it's a treat they appreciate to see such stock. It adds a sense of substance and permanency to the shop.

One additional device which sells books is something called a Torah Stand. This is an x-shaped stand of wood or plastic designed to hold a book in an open position. If you place one somewhere near the front of the store, open to show some lovely work of art, you'll be amazed how often you are forced to hunt up another colorful book to fill the empty stand. If you can't come up with a nice wooden one at a flea market they may be purchased from Brodart in plastic.

Now here's an important key to increased sales and customer satisfaction. The first hardback section the client should see upon entering your shop is one called NEW ARRIVALS. This is where your latest acquisitions get shelved as soon as they are priced. It gets them out of the way until you have time to put them in their various sections but that's not the real reason for it. Many of them will never reach their sections because they are going to sell right away. A very considerable portion of your business is going to come from a relatively small number of faithful regulars, perhaps no more than a hundred, who will visit your shop every few days or at least weekly. As a courtesy to these loyals I evolved this NEW ARRIVALS concept so they could duck in and see what was new in only a few minutes without having to canvas all their pet sections throughout the store. Then I made an interesting discovery. The idea that something is NEW, just arrived, makes it fascinating to people. Some dealers even go so far as to leave boxes of books around on the floor; they swear people are wild to go through them and they sell ten times faster than they would on the shelf. I have no reason to doubt it because when I'm buying or trading books it's often all I can do to stop customers from grabbing them before they're mine to sell. (I usually yell at them, "Back off — you're driving up the price!"). But personally I'm too obsessive-compulsive to tolerate boxes of books in the aisles. NEW ARRIVALS, however, is one of the best ideas I ever came up with. In order to make it even better, when the shelves aren't jammed full, select the most colorful and dramatic dust jackets and arrange these books facing outwards. It really moves them. It also makes it look as if you've got a lot more stock than you do. Next time you're in a new book store notice how well they make use of this gimmick.

If your shop has a stage area — a shallow built-up platform just inside the front windows — this is a great place to set up displays. Be creative! Use pyramids of those hollow plastic cubes, for instance. Do appropriate theme displays. Trust me; you can always come up with suitable books for any holiday I ever heard of. But keep it changing always. Dazzle them with mirrors. A couple of weeks is the most you should stick with any one display, with the notable exception of Christmas. No book should ever stay on NEW ARRIVALS even that long. You always feel as though you got away with something when you sell a book from NEW ARRIVALS. No wonder — it means you got out of having to file it.

While on the subject of properly displaying books, it is the custom of some poorly-operated shops to stack their paperbacks horizontally in little piles upon the shelves. This regrettable practice is sometimes justified under the theory that it is easier to read the titles and authors than if the books were vertical. There is a grain of truth in this, as there usually is in any misconception. I've yet to see a single truly successful store which displayed its books in this way. There are many counts against it: the books are gradually destroyed as they are removed and replaced from beneath the weight of other books, not even your most considerate customer is going to go to the trouble of keeping them in alphabetical order, and aesthetically it looks like hell. Suffice it to say, it is a lazy loser's way of doing things. Please never forget Rule #1 from Chapter 6: always maintain strict alphabetical order within each subject section. You absolutely cannot ignore this rule and succeed in this business. Certainly not on the scale we both intend that you should.

EASY-TO-DO REPAIRS WHICH YOU CAN PERFORM IN YOUR SHOP

In an earlier chapter I urged you not to shelve damaged books: i.e., those with broken hinges, stained or mildewed boards or loose pages. In most cases this is true, but there is a point at which it becomes logical to repair the books as opposed to rejecting them or tossing them in the trash. The point is naturally reached when the book's value is great enough, say fifteen or twenty dollars or more.

There are certain things you may become very proficient at and others which are impossible, or at least financially impractical. There's nothing you can do about missing pages or even pages with sections torn away. Badly chipped spines with the backing pieces missing may be repaired by an expert so that you'd hardly be able to tell but at a cost of over a hundred dollars this isn't much help for the average book. There are experts who can perform veritable miracles, reweaving paper, or even making paper from scratch. Book-binding is a fascinating and rewarding art, but let's confine this discussion to simple, easy repairs anyone can accomplish quickly.

Cracked, even broken, hinges may be tightened by the simple expedient of running a bead of Elmer's white glue along the inside of the spine. Stand the book upright, exposing the hollow between the spine and the backstrip by opening the pages widely. Deposit enough glue at the top so that it will run down the length of the spine. It will travel very slowly so that you may direct the glue right along the line of the crack in the binding. Just before it reaches the bottom, close the book and lay it upright, resting upon its spine, between opposing rows of books. It should be held tightly on both sides. If you've done your job well, within a couple of hours you will have a saleable book. It is well to not let the book sit too long before opening its covers for the first time; otherwise the repaired hinge may be so stiff they may not be able to be opened without further damage to the book.

Loose pages can usually be reinserted by simply touching a minute amount of glue to four or five points along the inside edge of the page and cracking the book wide to get the errant sheet far enough in so that it marries up with the rest when the book is closed. If this proves impossible you may have to trim the leading edge of the repaired page so that it doesn't protrude beyond the rest. There's no excuse for not matching it perfectly at top and bottom. Use glue ever so sparingly always.

Older books with sewn spines take the above repairs very well; more contemporary tomes whose spines are only glued are tougher and in some cases impossible. The sad truth is, they don't make them like they used to. Fortunately, most of the ones worth repairing are the older ones.

Now on to damaged boards and backstrips. Mildew is quite a common problem, the result usually of storing books in garages or basements without adequately protecting them against the ravages of damp. If the interior of the book is undamaged it is a simple matter of spraying the cover with any one of the many ammonia-based aerosol bathroom cleaners and wiping it off immediately. You must do the whole cover of the book, otherwise you'll never end up with a uniform color. The scent of the ammonia will be a bit much for a day or so but after that it will just smell fresh.

It is very often the case after the above repair that the cloth cover of the book will show lighter where the mildew was rampant. There are various other causes for discoloration of a cloth binding, principally water-spotting or other spills and sun fade.

When I bought my first shop I discovered a drawer containing twenty-two tins of shoe polish in the back room. Every color of the rainbow was included. I commented that someone must have quite an impressive collection of footwear but the ex-owner shook his head. No, he told me, that was his miracle drawer. He then plucked a book from a stack waiting to be repaired and proceeded to demonstrate. The book he'd selected was covered in red cloth. The boards were fine but the spine was faded to a shade much lighter, making the gilt title all but illegible. He rummaged around among the tins of shoe polish until he came up with one marked red. Using the usual stubby bristle brush, he liberally coated the spine of the book with red polish. Then he set it aside for about five minutes or so before taking an ordinary shoe buffer and removing the excess. He rubbed hard; when he was finished the title was much brighter against the now-darkened spine but the boards and spine still didn't quite match. Once again he began smearing on the polish, but this time covering the entire binding, spine and boards alike. Without waiting this time, he removed all the polish as soon as he was finished coating the outside of the book. Now the spine and boards were all but a perfect match as far as I could tell. He'd just turned a two dollar book into a ten dollar book as I stood watching. A pity few things in life are that simple or that rewarding.

If you elect to utilize any of the above repair techniques, practice on throw-away or at least inexpensive books until you get the hang of it. It's really just a matter of self-confidence and knowing what you can and cannot do. Be sure to do a thorough job of removing shoe polish from covers, otherwise your customers will wonder why their hands are covered with goo. It's a good idea to leave books treated with polish in the back room for a few days before shelving them.

Repairs on dust wrappers are simple and obvious and well worthwhile. Never shelve a book with a tear in the jacket; take a moment to tape it first. Naturally the tape goes on the inside of the wrapper. (Did you ever wonder how someone could be so stupid as to tape the OUTSIDE of a wrapper?)

Special rules apply to collectable book jackets. Never tape them if you can possibly avoid doing so. Remember, if the book is truly collectable you are going to be placing the jacket in a mylar cover anyway so no taping should be necessary. Many, in fact most, collectors are extremely reluctant to purchase a book with a repaired dust wrapper. I don't say some won't if the title is scarce enough but I've had little success selling such copies and when I have the price has had to be slashed far below that of a VG copy. Whenever you advertise or quote a repaired jacket you must tell the client it's a repaired jacket. Much better to tuck it as neatly and attractively as you can into a mylar cover and leave it alone.

Keep your eyes open as you move around your store, on the lookout for torn dust wrappers. Sometimes if the shelves are packed too tightly — a grievous sin which must be avoided — a wrapper will become damaged as the book is taken on and off for inspection. Take the time to stop and repair it when you see it. The hangdog sight of shabby dust wrappers detracts a great deal from the image you want to project. There comes a time in some cases when the jacket is too far gone to fool with and must be discarded. Be swift in doing so when that time comes.

We have confined our discussion to the repairing of hard-back books. Paperbacks require repairs as well but frankly I think you'll have better things to do. The newer, thicker pocket books are particularly prone to splitting down the spine and they are easy enough to glue but hopefully you're not going to have that kind of time to kill. Do what I do — toss them into the FREE box and forget it.

A LITTLE LOVING CARE FOR YOUR LEATHERBOUNDS

Books bound in leather or vellum are especially sought after by collectors and others who could normally care less about books. They are desirable as objects of art, decorations to highlight a room in home or office. Decorators sometimes ask for quotes on ''four feet of leatherbounds.'' It is one of the very few types of book I can think of which is often sold in spite of and not because of the contents.

Demand is especially fierce in the Midwest where old leatherbounds were never common and the ravages of weather have decimated many of those which did exist. There is a good living to be made by anyone who cares to make a career of shipping back such books from England, Scotland and a few other countries in Western Europe. It wasn't too terribly long ago there when the faithful family retainer would remove the leather books annually and treat them. Perhaps it's due to our classless society as much as anything that in this country such books are far more scarce.

That's the key, of course — care and conditioning. With the proper treatment such books may last hundreds of years. The paper had a very high rag content, far superior to our paper today. And the edge of each page was often gilt to protect the paper from acid decay. Did you ever wonder why all those guys were pushing those rickety carts around the streets in the period films set in the sixteenth to the nineteenth century? I mean the guys who were always yelling ''Rags, rags.'' Well they were gathering old clothes and whatever to be used to make paper, that's what they were doing. It was a thriving business. Starting with them and working up to the itinerant bookseller who carried his total stock in his pocket, all the way to the publisher, there were an astounding number of people engaged in the book industry. (How did you think we struggled out of the Dark Ages?)

Back to leatherbounds. Leather is, after all, animal tissue. It is prone to deteriorate, though cool temperatures and moderate humidity ameliorate this. Much has to do with how the skin was cured and tanned in the first place but there isn't a whole lot you can do about that. What you can do is keep a jar of neat's foot oil at hand to treat your hidebound books from time to time. Neat's foot oil is an oil taken from the foot of cattle. You should be able to find it in any fine leather shop. It's contained in conventional boot and saddle treatments, along with lanolin, and these may be used as well.

One of the indescribable joys of this business is that of holding in your hand an early seventeenth century leatherbound in nearly perfect condition. That's when you find out whether you're a bookseller first or a collector. The urge to take it home is nearly overwhelming. It's a tough call but the nice thing about it is, either way you win.

13

On the Importance of Being Happy As Well As Prosperous

The most hostile critic is bound to admit that the frater-
nity of bibliophiles is eminently picturesque. If their doings
are inscrutable, they are also romantic; if their vices are
numerous, the heinousness of those vices is mitigated by the
fact that it is possible to sin humorously. Regard him how
you will, the sayings and doings of the collector give life and
color to the pages of those books which treat of books.

Leon H. Vincent

YOUR SHOP'S PERSONALITY

Have I mentioned that all of this is designed to be fun, too? Well it is, if you do it right. In fact it's a ball! (With the notable exception of the initial construction work. That, I freely admit, is no party unless you happen to be a devout masochist.)

You should scarcely be able to wait to get those doors open in the morning. Why not? Within the very first year you should be earning as much money as the average doctor, way more than the average lawyer, and as much as most big city mayors without all the soul-sapping stress and abuse they have to bear. You're dealing with a product you presumably love; your clientele is the pick of the buying public. And just what is your shop's personality? Why, it's yours, of course!

Every bookseller has his or her special loves. With me it's mysteries, science fiction and illustrated books. (Three of the better loves to have from a commercial standpoint.) Inevitably your shop will reflect these proclivities and it is well it should. You'll be more prone to seek out and acquire material from other dealers, the AB and catalogues, if it appeals to you personally. You'll be more successful at promoting and selling books when your own interest in them is genuine. If you are attracted to a subject you will gladly seek out and likely retain more knowledge and history of it than if you have to force it. The whole thing becomes a sort of a fantasy-fulfilling experience. Many's the time I've stood in my shop surrounded by fifty or sixty thousand books and revelled in the realization that it was remarkably like one of my fondest childhood daydreams. How can you beat a career requiring you to do just what you'd most like to be doing anyway: seeking and procuring books you are fascinated with. Some will be books you might never have seen or have been able to afford otherwise. Now you spend your days amongst them, enjoying them at least for a time, while making an excellent living in the bargain. (What you do for a living is in fact what many readers dream of doing on their days off or when they retire.)

To be brutally honest, though, there is another side to this golden coin. There are times it nearly breaks your heart to part with certain books. I speak of the truly scarce ones you have to know you will never see, much less possess, again. Here you will be faced with a decision: you will have to decide whether you're first a bookseller or a collector. It's your option. I know many a dealer who is happy to scale down his income a little in order to enhance his own private collection and there isn't a thing in the world wrong with that.

The average-sized shop laid out within these pages is going to have just about one hundred subject sections, but still that shop is going to develop a distinct personality within a very short time. It would be nice, however, if your own areas of interest weren't too esoteric or inappropriate. I mean, it wouldn't be very productive to devote a lot of space to Islamic Culture if you opened your shop in a small town in the Midwest.

One of the happiest, thriving shops I know is one run by a mother and her two daughters. They are all Harlequin buffs and this is the long suit featured within their shop. God, how the ladies flock in there, chattering about this and that writer and grabbing books by the armfuls. And the owners know exactly what their customers are talking about and can answer questions which come up. Frankly, to me it's enough to gag a goat but for them it's beautiful and that's the system working at its best.

There's another small pleasure I believe you should allow yourself, within reason. If there's a topic, subject or certain type of book which deeply offends you — don't stock it! There are a few such categories I've passed on offering in any of my stores. From time to time the policy has cost me some sales but I'm satisfied with the tradeoff. My list of personal no-no's includes survivalist manuals showing how to make bombs out of common materials found in the home and one hundred and one ways to kill your fellow man, as well as what is commonly known as "adult" books. Sure, you must serve your customers' needs but that doesn't mean you have to abrogate your own set of values.

Just don't get too carried away. You must resist the urge, should you have it, to be judgmental concerning other peoples' reading habits. To do so is stupid, self-defeating and downright silly. But you do have the right and the obligation to your own self-esteem to draw the line wherever you feel you must.

Before leaving the subject of your shop's personality, I want to impress upon you the importance of being a good listener. It's an uncommon gift. It's the first thing I always tried to teach incoming salespeople when I trained them in the pharmaceutical industry. Everything you will ever have to know about the world of books you will learn from your customers. And, oh, how they'll love you for listening. Collectors acquire enormous funds of information about their own little narrow fields of interest. They spend their lives searching for someone to tell some of it to. It's your opportunity to acquire what amounts to a graduate degree in a whole range of subjects. I had a customer once who knew the full and complete details of every battle and skirmish in the Civil War. I mean names, dates, weather conditions, you name it and he knew it. As a result I can now pass myself off in a pinch as something of an authority on the Civil War. The same is true of dozens of other subjects ranging from gardening to metaphysics; subjects I would have never dreamed of reading up on but now have a fair working knowledge of. Remember the old joke about the guy who talked on and on, while the second man mutely listened, nodding his head once in a while? When the first guy left he remarked that the second fellow was the brightest person he'd met in ages. It's true — the only substitute for intelligence is silence. So just listen and they'll love you for it.

It isn't just collectors who educate you. Avid readers will keep you up to date on the pros and cons of the latest potboilers, mysteries and historical romances. These are all things it's helpful to know. You can't reasonably be expected to have read but a small fraction of the books within your shop but somehow the customers assume you have. You'll be constantly asked to recommend books or for your opinion of titles or authors. If you're a good listener you'll soon be fielding those queries handily even though you've never read them yourself. A common plea is from the reader who has read everything a certain author has written and is now at a loss. He wants to know who writes like this author. You won't score any points by passing on the question so you're going to have to tell him something. If you make an active effort to listen it won't be a problem. Skills such as listening may be acquired. Once set, it becomes automatic and a never-ending source of knowledge.

BE ALL THINGS TO ALL PEOPLE — AND FAIL!

If you've never been in business for yourself before you're in for a revelation. So far we've discussed mostly positive aspects of business and saying yes a lot. Now it's time to talk about saying no.

I'm certain it's worse in just about any small business you might name but even so the book business has its pitfalls. Most of them are too obvious to mention but a few are more subtle and I want to spell them out for you. Perhaps the most insidious is the practice of accepting books for sale on consignment. On the face of it you may think it sounds a wonderful arrangement: having a collection of fine books to sell without having to dole out the money for them until they're sold. NEVER accept books on consignment. If they are that hot, buy them. If cash is a problem in the beginning, establish a line of credit with your bank to cover extraordinary purchases of fine libraries. But never under any circumstances accept a book in your shop unless you own it outright. It's brought nothing but grief to any number of friends in the business. In at least one case I know of it ended up a nasty case in court which ended up costing the shop owner far more than any profit realized from the consignment books. There's just something about the whole concept of consignment which seems prone to turn sour every time. I guess it's because it's a contract but it's an unfulfilled contract; as any broker or attorney will tell you, that's simply trouble waiting to happen. The problem is people change their minds and time dulls the initial enthusiasm for almost any deal struck. Just trust me on this one; it's been a thorn in the side of everyone I know of who ever got involved with it.

Then you'll get the earnest folks who just know you'll make a mint if you stock _____. You can fill in the blank with anything from greeting cards to comic books. People will come in your shop from time to time looking for greeting cards but don't get carried away. I've seen shops squeeze in racks of cards to try and boost the gross and it's never worked that I heard of. What it does do is make you look desperate and foolish. Now you're faced with the problem of attracting the attention of two widely disparate groups of buyers and you're in a diminished position to serve either one. As for comic books, I've got nothing against them except I can't ever remember seeing a nice antiquarian book shop with comic books in it. Again, I think it's two different worlds but on this I could be wrong. Comics are hot; there are one hell of a lot of zealous comic collectors around. Maybe I just can't get excited about the product.

There are plenty of other things they'll either try to foist off on you or ask you to begin stocking for their benefit. Old post cards is one which comes up periodically. Magazines is the most common. If you want to die of a broken heart, try being a used periodical dealer. You start out with a large warehouse and and even bigger checkbook just so you can be sure and have that one certain issue someone will eventually ask for. Meanwhile your stock will disintegrate under the assault of handling and everyone will want to know why in the hell your prices are so high.

A good friend of mine with a fine store in Southern California is a real pigeon for all these things. God love him, he's undoubtedly saved me thousands of dollars and untold aggravation by testing all these things out instead of me. I've watched him go through magazines, cards, games, tapes of old radio shows, maps, new books. The only one of the above which wasn't an unmitigated disaster was the old radio tapes — I think he nearly broke even on those. His store thrives but I guess he's just one of those nice guys who hates to say no. The sad part about it isn't just that he fails to make any money on the other stock; it's that each time he has to clear out large numbers of books in order to make room and then his sales fall off because he hasn't got the stock.

I guess by now you're beginning to get the idea. Be the best bookseller you can and let someone else carry on the experiments with grief.

SERVING YOUR CUSTOMERS' NEEDS IS ALL THERE IS TO IT

If the above is an oversimplification it isn't much of one. As I've alluded to from time to time, I've been involved in and owned a handful of businesses. The book business is the only one I've ever known where it wasn't necessary to think in terms of money, income, or profit first. I suppose I did in the beginning of course, but once I saw what was happening, what the numbers looked like, I forgot all about that and just enjoyed myself. It's a rare and wonderful boon in this day and age to be able to do that: just concentrate on genuinely meeting the needs of your clients the best you possibly can, relaxed in the knowledge that the rest really will take care of itself. In turn the clients sense this joy and commitment and how they respond to it. Why shouldn't they? When was the last time you went into a retail store and picked up on that kind of attitude? It's a fantastic circle of service, respect, joy and satisfaction; I hope you join the club.

It became common soon after I opened each of my stores for certain customers to drop in on a regular basis. Some began calling it their "haven." Others assured me if not for the half hour of tranquility they found in my shop each day they didn't think they'd make it. College students used to come in with their chess board and play endless games. Walking into my shop is like walking into the home of your best friend. No pretenses required. One of my best customers used to like to sit on the floor while she thumbed through her potential purchases. One day I told her it was nice to see how relaxed and obviously at home she felt in my store. She beamed and told me I certainly had a different attitude than the guy who ran a shop four times the size of mine in the same city. It seems she'd pulled her sitting on the floor routine there and the owner told her she couldn't do that. When I asked her why she said she had no idea. To this day I've never been able to figure out why he'd take exception to it. I think it's the best way I know to illustrate my point though. I think it gives you a clue why I did considerably more business in my store than the other fellow did with four times the space and books. (He once asked me at a booksellers' association meeting how I managed to do so much business at my shop and I told him I let the customers sit on the floor. He looked at me like I was nuts.)

What I'm trying to tell you is, relax and be a nice guy — it's fun! Don't be stupid like some dealers I've seen and insult your customers at the same time you're rejecting their trades. It is necessary to reject more books than you accept but it's easy to do it in such a way that you don't offend. Explain why you're unable to accept the rejects: they're too worn or they're underlined or you already have too many or those subjects don't sell or whatever. If a customer is one of my really heavy buyers I've been known to take their trades, only to toss them into the free box as soon as they leave. And never succumb to the all-too-common disease of this and many another business — elitism. As time goes on and you come to know so very much about the used book business there is a tendency to look upon your clients as mental deficients. You see a lot of it in this industry. People ask you to order out-of-print books as if it were only a matter of calling a wholesaler; many don't know the difference between fiction and non-fiction. Please remember how angry you've felt when someone else put you in that position and resolve never to sink to it. Why should they know did-dly squat about the antiquarian book business? That's why you're making the big bucks, isn't it? Because you're the expert. They are probably absolute whiz bangs at whatever it is they do, so be nice. There's a hard-ware store where I live that has the most extensive stock in town. I'm sometimes forced to go there if I can't find what I want elsewhere but I'll go to any lengths to avoid it. The reason is simply the elitist bastard who runs the place. He always finds some way to let you know you're a fool and he's the expert. It's a sick game I'm sorry to say quite a few of the antiquarian booksellers are prone to play. It's something which seems to come with success but you'll never convince me it isn't a clear sign of low self-esteem. Maybe realizing that fact will help you steer clear of it.

Don't be afraid to kid your customers outrageously after you get to know them. Most people love it! It's the sort of camaraderie you see within really close families. There's too little of it now and I think people miss it. We all tend to treat people we don't like with strict formality; razzing the hell out of somebody is a clear message of affection. Of course there will be those you won't want to use this approach with but they're easily spotted. They usually have faces carved from hardwood and their eyes have all the sparkle of a firefly in August.

I can't begin to list all the wonderful kindnesses my clients have done for me over the years. Some were big things such as getting me lots of free publicity in the local paper; some were small things like bringing me paper bags so I wouldn't have to buy them. (I once got disgusted at the high price of paper bags, so I asked a few of the ladies if they had any extras they could bring in to me. Word spread and I was soon filling the dumpster behind the store with tons of paper bags I didn't need.) Many's the time I've gone to my shop in the morning to find cases of books sitting on the sidewalk for me. Donations from some satisfied customer.

The old saw about casting your bread upon the waters may be considered archaic in some circles but it still holds true in the book business. A lot of old values and truisms do. It's a part of the wonderful heritage of bookselling.

14

What If
That Book
Doesn't Sell?

Never try to force a book. If it can't talk back to you, or better make you talk back to it, don't feel guilty about it—put it aside. If it's a great book you'll just have to grow up to it, and you will if you keep yourself in motion. A man has to have a dialogue with a good book and with a lot of such books you just don't become man enough to read them with profit until you've grown up to them.

J. Frank Dobie

KEEPING THE DEADWOOD OFF YOUR SHELVES

One of the most common pitfalls in this business occurs after you've been operating from six months to a year. Your shelves have filled; there's a tendency to slack way off on buying and trading and just rely on current stock to carry you along. Don't do it! You've absolutely got to maintain that sense of excitement, that ''something's always going on here'' atmosphere which is what made you successful in the first place.

There is something important I learned from a man named Joe. Joe is a fascinating fellow who's been a bookseller longer than I've been alive. His store stands three stories and contains a quarter-million books. From time to time the local paper likes to run a story on Joe, usually titled, ''The Man Who Remembers Everything'' or something similar. In reality he's pretty weak on names but the impressive thing is whenever someone asks for a certain book he's able to dart off, upstairs or down, and quickly return bearing the title. One of the things Joe loves about this business is he figures there aren't too many where he could leave a dish of change on the counter with a note saying, "Gone next door for lunch. Make your own change." Last time I saw Joe he was seventy-four and still going strong. He likes to get in a game of tennis in the mornings before opening and he loves to go out dancing a couple of nights a week. You've no doubt noticed people who truly love their lives often seem semi-indestructible.

The important thing Joe taught me is that there's a simple device which serves the same purpose as does the vulture in the desert. It's called a bargain rack and it keeps your shelves clean. Every morning old Joe would tote his two-tiered rack out onto the sidewalk in front of his shop and fill it with his mistakes. Sure he was still making them — so will you! The sign on the rack reads "3 For $1.00" and as the day wore on he would add to it as space became available.

Without some such device any used book store is in imminent danger of becoming a stale, dull place. I've seen uncountable numbers of shops it's happened to. The bargain rack is where you go to admit your mistakes and confession is good for the soul. (It's also great for business.) The fodder for the rack might be books you should never have bought in the first place. Sometimes you get busy and you fail to check as closely as you should; you end up with nice books which are highlighted or underlined. To the rack with them! Never put a defaced book on your shelf in the shop. And when you get sick of looking at a book which has sat on your shelf for two years, how do you think your customers feel? When you find yourself in the position of having to swallow a bitter pill the best thing to do is make it quick and get it over with. To the rack with it!

It is quite common for people to leave behind those books which you've rejected for purchasing or accepting in trade. Some of these will have sufficient merit to make it to the rack. Don't put the real junk out there though; set it aside in the back room. Later in this chapter I'll show you how to make a profit on it, too.

Never regard that bargain rack as a symbol of defeat — far from it. First of all, it's nearly pure profit. Most of the books which go out there were either left behind for free or you traded for them. In either case you have little or no investment tied up in them. You're never going to put out a twenty-five dollar book just because it's been sitting too long. What you'll do is drop the price to maybe fifteen dollars in order to move it.

That innocuous-looking rack represents several thousand dollars in bonus money annually. More importantly, it increases the productivity of your store tremendously by keeping that fresh look about your stock. It also stops people in their tracks who might otherwise never think to enter your shop. Few can resist such a bargain, especially when it's right there on the walk within arm's reach. And they must come inside to pay for them. Stop and think: getting people inside your store like that is what most retailers spend a fortune on ads and giveaways to accomplish. You've got 'em paying you to come inside. The rack also serves to let passing motorists know whether or not the shop is open. At least it does if you are visible from the street. An OPEN or CLOSED sign is usually unable to be read from the street but they can see that rack. Finally, it suggests to the public the fact that there are indeed very real values inside as well as outside. All this while generating a handsome little stipend you wouldn't otherwise have.

So much for the disposition of the hardback losers. What about the paperbacks? I've seen many a store offer them at from five to ten for a dollar and it's a terrible mistake. I realize it's somewhat the same principle I was just waxing so enthusiastic over with the hardbound books but there's a big difference. Stated in its simplest terms: displaying and offering for sale anything that cheap looks bad and displaying paperbacks which are much short of Fine detracts terribly from the attractiveness and appeal of your shop.

I've found a better way of utilizing these shabby or outdated pocket books. In each of my shops I've constructed a small shallow box — about 2 ft. x 3 ft. x 4'' deep — where I place them. The sign on the front of the box reads, ''One Free With Purchase.'' The books wouldn't generate all that much income but what a crop of good will they bring. You'll get a kick out of seeing the looks of surprise and suspicion and satisfaction on your customers' faces the first time they realize they are actually free to take another book at no cost. It's a strange thing, but I've never seen another antiquarian shop with a FREE box. Most just throw them away. Now I throw away any which have missing pages or mildew or stink of tobacco smoke but I haven't the heart to toss out perfectly readable, intact books; it just doesn't seem right. I used to donate them to a local juvenile detention facility, but then I got the impression they considered my calls to come pick up a batch as more of a nuisance than anything else so I decided to direct my philanthropical efforts toward my favorite group in the world — my customers. It's a wonderful little system: it makes them feel good and it makes me feel great. I recommend you do it, too. Feed the box with those paperbacks left behind after being rejected and become brutal about plucking stale stock off the shelf and tossing it into the box as well.

There is a stupid and deadly philosophy rampant within this industry. I'd venture to say it's among the top three reasons so many shops never achieve much more than mediocrity in sales volume. It's a sick sort of stubborn elitism which prevents dealers from learning from their mistakes or misconceptions, stops them from adjusting to the conditions which prevail before doing serious damage to their businesses. I've been around long enough to be able to walk into some shops and see some of the same stock I've seen as much as a decade ago. Hard to believe, I know, but it's true. In such shops it is also common to find some sort of code written in along with the price. The code tells the dealer what he paid for that book. Use of the code is often accompanied by the insane determination to sell that particular book at a profit come hell or high water.

My advice is to forget what you paid for a book as soon as possible after pricing it. If you've got the brains God gave a gnat you'll soon realize it doesn't make a tinker's dam what price you get for a given book; all that matters is your overall profit margin and the steady growth of your sales. I assure you I never think about it but rest assured I've sold books for less than I paid for them. I couldn't tell you how many — I haven't a clue — but the point is I SOLD THEM! I didn't let them sit on the shelf and ossify and become a symbol of ennui to my clients. I didn't leave that money tied up in one book for years; instead I converted it back into cash and bought more books which I converted into cash and bought more books, etc.

The book business, like many another, I suspect, has an important factor of timing. There's that first burst of excitement when a new book hits the shelf; it often sells within a week or two. Then comes the normal shelf life of from three to six months, followed by a downhill slide into becoming a liability instead of an asset. What does a new bookstore owner do when a book doesn't sell? He returns it to the publisher for a refund. You can't do that with your mistakes, but you've got to do something. Whatever is appropriate, the bargain rack, the FREE box or a price reduction, do it when the time comes. If you've got a lot of Scottish blood in you it may come hard at first but hopefully you can understand and appreciate the logic expressed above.

The foregoing statements apply to all levels of stock but the time elements, six months, refers to general stock. It may well take longer to sell your top-of-the-line material, say books ranging upwards of two or three hundred dollars. I wouldn't panic if this material sits for a year or two, but there comes a time even with these when adjustments must be made. If I offer fine material in an AB ad and it doesn't sell and it's been around for a year or so, I'd definitely lower the price. Use your common sense. Highly unusual, esoteric material takes longer to sell than signed first editions of some "hot" writer. Be more patient with really scarce books; chances are when a buyer hoves in sight his decision won't be based primarily on price. You can only shop price when other identical units are available.

Another thing you have to watch is the constant changing of readers' tastes. Certain genres tend to ebb and flow and in some cases nearly disappear altogether. The amount of shelf space you allocate to any given subject or area of fiction should directly match the current demand. This is a lesson I learned the hard way. About a decade ago one of the most active sections in my store was Gothic Romances. It's easy to spot a Gothic: there's always a castle in the background. It was difficult to keep up with the demand it was so great. Then gradually my Gothic section began to swell, blossoming forth into surrounding sections. I kept buying, happy in the knowledge that for once I'd have an adequate supply. About the time they threatened to overrun the entire fiction section a friend who was a new book dealer told me the new, more sexually explicit romances had blown Gothics right out of the water. Gothics were dead, and remain so to this day. It was an expensive lesson but those are the best kind — the ones you pay cash for. Frequent visits to one of your local new book shops will educate you concerning contemporary trends and new directions. Actually most genres such as science fiction, mysteries and westerns are pretty constant but others, such as romances, can be very volatile.

When all is said and done, still the best way to keep the deadwood off your shelves is not to accept it in the first place. We've covered the subject pretty thoroughly in previous chapters, but since it's one of the vital rules of success it bears repeating. You may get by with violating some of the precepts I've layed down but this one is certain death if ignored. It's particularly dangerous due to the simple fact that the very books you must avoid are the ones you'll be most commonly offered. Again, they are: outdated novels, especially book clubs or copies without wrappers, Reader's Digest Condensed Books, outdated references on things like banking, real estate or stocks, non-sellers such as political science, economics and social science, education, books concerning the First World War, books about UFO's, old sets of encyclopedias, all but the most contemporary of travel books, all but the most recent of health and diet books, and biographies of little-known and long-forgotten people. This list is by no means complete and must be fleshed out to fit the needs of your particular area, but it does cover the worst of the "deadwood" and should save you a good deal of wasted effort and lost revenue.

MAKING MONEY BY GIVING BOOKS AWAY

Even utilizing the methods outlined above, you're still going to be left with a constantly-growing supply of totally unsaleable hardback books. Paperbacks aren't going to be a problem except for times when so many rejects pile up that your FREE box can't dispense them fast enough. For the most part it will be hardbacks which will accumulate in your storage area. These will consist of books which aren't even worthy of space in your bargain rack. They will be just the kinds of books outlined earlier in this chapter. Yes, they'll find their way into your shop somehow, in spite of all your best efforts. One way they arrive is as part of a library purchase where you had to buy it on an "all-or-nothing" basis. Sellers will sometimes do this and it is wise of them to do so; otherwise a dealer will skim the cream off the offering, leaving them with the same problem of disposal they start-ed with. Of course you will predicate the price you pay upon the desirable material and pay nothing for the junk titles.

Nevertheless, you'll soon find yourself warehousing a surprising number of trash books. You must keep your limited storage area clear, ready to receive the next large batch of good material. Fortunately there's a way to do this and actually make money at the same time.

Whenever you have a full load for whatever vehicle you use as your com-pany car, throw in the losers you've culled from your shelves or somehow accumulated and take them to the nearest non-profit thrift store. It may be a Salvation Army retail store or a Christian Thrift Shop or an Amvets or whatever. Donate the books to them, but be sure you get someone in management to SIGN A RECEIPT for them. List the number of books donated, designate them hardback or paperback, and have the person signing designate his position with the firm. Now don't bother trying to get them to place a value on the donated merchandise — they won't do it. That's entirely up to you. The key here is to be reasonable and fair; if you should ever be audited, the figures you assign your donations will have to stand up under scrutiny. The obvious figure to use is that which the store will be attempting to sell them for, usually something on the order of fifty cents per hardback and twenty-five cents per pocket book. The tax code says to use your cost as a basis for value; this is difficult to do in our business, but the modest values mentioned above should be more than fair. The books you have no money in should offset those for which you may have paid more than the per book value assigned.

If this all sounds like small potatoes to you, think again! The last year I owned and operated a retail shop I enjoyed a donation deduction of twenty-five thousand dollars right off the top ; and that, friends, is one very nice-sized potato. A thriving store will amass an amazing amount of these overly-common books and it's well worth your time and trouble to make intelligent use of them.

You will also be enjoined to make donations to various charitable community fund-raisers, as well as to libraries and schools. I don't always respond favorably to such requests but often I do and the same principles apply. The difference is you will want to match the gift to the cause. You wouldn't want to make yourself look a fool by giving a case of old textbooks to be auctioned off at a local charity telethon. If it's a school I usually send a set of older encyclopedias or history or geography sets, something I'm getting tired of looking at anyway but attractive and having some value. If it's more of a posh affair like a charity auction I select something in a nice matched binding, say a set of the complete works of R.L. Stevenson. Your deduction may be based upon a percentage of the auction price, which is likely to exceed your retail. A combination thank-you note and receipt showing price realized should be sent to you.

In view of the above, you may imagine my chagrin when I'm in other dealers' shops and they insist people remove their rejected books. If the books are damp with mildew or really rotten I do the same, but failing that I'm happy to allow them to be left behind. I tell people exactly what I will do with them and they are invariably relieved not to have to lug them back home. I suppose I shouldn't be surprised; obviously these dealers don't have any tax problems to worry about. But you are going to, so please do both yourself and your customers a favor and let them leave the culls behind. They are, quite literally, money in the bank.

15

If You Love to Travel, You're in Luck

Some books are to be read in a hour, and returned to the shelf; others require a lifetime to savor their richness. Such books should be owned in personal copies, to travel with and to sleep beside—the most fruitful of all companions. Only your bookseller can consummate such a union of book and reader.

Lawrence Clark Powell

BOOKSELLERS MAY ENJOY VERY PROFITABLE VACATIONS

It's true the majority of even the more successful antiquarian shop owners never go on buying trips. It really isn't necessary. But if you are the peripatetic type and dream of traveling cross country or going foreign, the business lends itself to that avocation very well. Assuming the fact you've developed reliable staff to cover for you, the world is indeed your oyster.

A friend of mine in California is a native of Holland. Each spring he makes a pilgrimage back home. Along the way he spends some time in England and Scotland, invariably shipping back many cases of wonderful books. You might imagine how his clients look forward to examining the newly-arrived treasure trove each summer. His stock is the envy of every other dealer in the area. He takes full advantage of the simple premise of importing: he buys desirable material where it is common and sells it where it is uncommon. The fine leatherbounds he comes home with are quickly snatched up by avid collectors on the West Coast where such books are scarce.

It makes for an ideal situation: he is able to write off the cost of a marvelous trip most people would love to make and makes a handsome profit into the bargain. His shop is so impressive he was recently awarded membership in the illustrious Antiquarian Booksellers Association of America.

Perhaps the most enjoyable and productive domestic trip for the average general stock dealer is to wander through New England in late spring or early summer. Perhaps because that area of the country is older, there always seems to be an abundance of fine material to be found. The most marvelous shops abound. There are even great book barns; actual barns converted to book shops full of hundreds of thousands of books which are often available at comparatively low prices. These places almost operate as wholesalers because of the ease with which they may restock and the rather limited season nature imposes upon them. Often they are set up so that all books in a given section are uniformly priced; I know of at least one such operation which sells books at so much the box. A trip such as this can reap very large dividends for those of us whose shops are located in areas where fine books are not so plentiful. You certainly earn the admiration and gratitude of your customers when you return with some of those precious titles they've lusted for. Needless to say, you go on such trips armed with a shopping list. The real bonus is you are enjoying a terrific trip which most people pay the travel agencies dearly for. There isn't a thing devious about it either; it is a valid business trip by any standard. (Just don't come home without any books).

To me, this is one of the great fringe benefits which accrues to you as your business flourishes. This is one of the payoffs for your burgeoning knowledge and the work that went into acquiring it. If you love seeing new places and meeting wonderful people you really should consider pursuing this exciting phase of the industry.

We all develop our favorite patterns and places to travel so I won't attempt to give specific advice on itineraries. I find that I tend to follow pretty well-established routes myself. Part of the reason is that I've already separated the wheat from the chaff along those routes and then there's the added bonus of seeing old friends.

Some dealers swear they can accomplish more by just covering the many and varied book stores of New York City than they can chasing across the country. I'm certain that's entirely true but it's not for me. Personally I shudder with horror at the very thought of spending any time at all within that vast teeming mob.

So inevitably will your own personality dictate where you'll want to travel on your shopping sprees. Here's some food for thought though: I can't deny fine antiquarian shops will have a far greater offering of scarce material on hand. And it's true such stores exist almost exclusively in moderate to large communities. But it's also true such stores tend to be quite sophisticated when it comes to pricing their books and what's the point in finding the books if you can't afford to buy them?

Smaller stores found in smaller communities have desirable books as well; perhaps not in profusion but such material comes their way whether they seek it and understand it or not, merely through the laws of chance. Better yet, many of these stores aren't much concerned with collectable books and don't cater to collectors, only to readers looking for bargains. Most of them don't even own any price guides, nor do they subscribe to the AB. They don't know — and may not even care — that there are books on their shelves priced at a few dollars which are worth a hundred.

I once found a F copy of Poul Anderson's *Three Hearts For Three Lions* on the shelf of a tiny book store located in a small town of eight thousand. It was priced at one dollar. As I paid for it I couldn't resist telling the owner that I'd be selling the book for at least seventy-five dollars and suggested that he invest in an inexpensive price guide and make himself aware of such collectable material. He merely laughed and shook his head. He assured me there weren't enough collectors in his town to worry about and he was happy to receive a dollar for the book. Based upon what he'd paid for it he was realizing his full profit. Then he opined that while I was fooling around trying to sell one book for seventy-five dollars he'd easily sell seventy-five books for a dollar each and figure he had the better of the bargain.

He'd made his point; we parted friends, each convinced we were the cleverer of the two. As I've stated before, it certainly isn't necessary to get deeply involved with collectable books in order to operate a thriving shop. If it so happens you live in a community of fewer than, say, forty thousand people and you elect to open a shop, it may be more effort than it's worth to even try. But you will miss out on much of the thrill and excitement of the book business and since a large part of your collectable business will be conducted via the mails, location is not much of a deterrent.

There is a proper etiquette which should always be followed when entering another dealer's shop. Begin by introducing yourself to the owner if he or she is available; or if not, to whomever is on duty. Inquire about the store's policy concerning discounts to the trade. Most stores will offer the standard 20 per cent. There are a few from which I receive 30 per cent but this is based on a long-standing relationship. I have found a few stores which offer a niggardly 10 per cent. Inform the owner which subject sections you would like to peruse; you can waste a good deal of time getting oriented in a strange store. It also gives the owner the opportunity to bring out any gems he may be keeping under wraps. I think it's a good idea to always ask if there are any fine books not on display. On half a dozen occasions that question has resulted in an invitation to the proprietor's home and the acquisition of some of the finest treasures I've ever owned. It is very common for store owners to hold back special material, especially very old books and ephemera which requires careful handling. I suppose it's the result of having had a bad experience in the shop when someone damaged an old book through inattention or mishandling.

Don't be shy about making offers on books you want. If you find some of the types of material you want but the price is such that you couldn't make a reasonable profit, explain the situation and ask whether he might not consider a somewhat larger discount. The more you are willing to buy the better your chances are of getting this consideration. Be careful to couch your request in such a way that there is never a suggestion he has priced his books too high. Even if you DO think it, his pricing policies are entirely his own and it's not for you to question them. More often than not he will accede to your request. For all you know he may have been about to slash the prices anyway. I nearly always agree to such requests myself, depending upon the way it's put and, of course, on the amount and the type of material involved.

When your purchase is completed you are left with the problem of getting the books home. Always carry shipping materials with you in your car. The store owner may be relied upon to supply boxes. Bring in your materials and pack your own books, not because you don't trust the dealer to ship the books, nothing to worry about there. You should do it because the odds are far too good he doesn't know how to pack books properly for shipping and you'll want them to arrive in the same condition as when you bought them. Depending upon circumstances, you may take the boxes with you and mail them or you may leave them along with adequate funds for the seller to ship.

Never forget that when you're going to all the trouble of making a valuable contact like this it would be foolish not to take full advantage of the situation by attempting to establish an ongoing relationship. By the time you've managed to break away from your shop and travel you should have developed a permanent want list showing the kinds of material you will always be interested in acquiring. A copy of this permanent want list should be included every time you ship a book to another dealer. You should have handed one of them to the bookseller you just bought those books from. He'll never be more well-inclined toward you than he is right then; you've just made what for him may be a memorable purchase. Ask him to place your list where he can see it and remember it, to please drop you a quote whenever he gets material he thinks is suitable. It's true most of them will never be heard from again but others will, thus establishing a valued pipeline for your continuing supply of exceptional books. There are some highly-respected dealers who enjoy the almost mythical reputation of always having far more than their share of superb offerings on hand. This is certain to be the result of regular road trips or such liasons established at a time when they did travel.

The vast majority of booksellers are great people. Many lasting friendships develop. I actually only recall being treated rudely once by a peer and that was in San Francisco, which must by all accounts be considered a rude city anyway. It was one of those terribly, terribly posh shops where owner and employees were dressed to the nines and incredibly impressed with themselves for reasons not apparent to me. In all fairness, let me hasten to add I was received with great charm and courtesy in every other shop I visited in the City By The Bay.

These book buying trips needn't be either lengthy or expensive. My wife, Patti, recently returned from a trip to Texas. The journey was for the purpose of visiting friends. During the course of a ten day trip she devoted something under five hours to buying books. It soon becomes unthinkable for a dealer to visit anywhere without checking out book shops, thrift stores, etc.. She came home with several hundred dollars worth of books for which she had spent the total sum of just under thirty dollars. Since she was staying with friends she actually showed a profit for the trip by simply investing a few pleasant hours visiting a couple of shops.

BOOK FAIRS — A BOOKSELLER'S DREAM COME TRUE!

Your first visit to a book fair will be a lot like a child's first trip to Disney World. It really is the ultimate experience for any serious dealer or collector. You'll find yourself surrounded by kindred spirits and more fabulous books than you can ever begin to appreciate. NEVER miss an opportunity to attend one, even if it means traveling some considerable distance. There is no better way to recharge your bookselling batteries, not to mention finding many of those hard-to-find titles on your want list. (Before you leave it's a good idea to contact those clients with the more expensive wants and get them to authorize you to spend up to a specific limit to acquire their books.)

In any case, don't neglect to bring your checkbook. Though it's true dealers who are displaying tend to price their books on the high side for fairs I've yet to come away from one without at least a case full. Fairs are no different than shops, after all; each dealer prices his own wares. You'll discover a price variation of as much as 50 per cent on identical books being offered at the same fair. Fair committees commonly limit dealers to giving only a 10 per cent discount to the trade, so there isn't much flexibility on prices. (On the final fair day, when dealers are faced with the gloomy prospect of lugging all the unsold books home again, prices tend to become much more flexible.) It is also common for dealers to do a lot of trading among themselves toward the close of a fair. Each attempts to swap off those books which are alien to their special interests for some which are more appropriate.

A fair is a real crash course in bookselling. There is no possible way you could come away not knowing one hell of a lot more than when you went in, I don't care how long you've been in the business. You'll be able to see books you've only heard about, multitudes of material you've never seen before and may never again. You'll enjoy a lot of input concerning other dealers' ideas on pricing of books you may have in stock or that you deal in regularly. You'll have the opportunity to exchange information with experts in areas of the industry you may not have even known existed.

Use the golden moment to introduce yourself around. Hand out business cards, along with a copy of your own permanent want list. Remember to bring along a very sturdy shopping bag to hold all the permanent want lists and catalogues you'll acquire as you make the rounds. This is called networking and nobody does it better than antiquarian booksellers. You'll be invited to sign up to receive other dealers' regular mailings; do so unless their theme is totally foreign to your business.

Naturally you'll seek out those displays which touch upon your own interests. That's all well and good, but please don't neglect the ones which are alien to you. Stop, look, and learn from that booth dealing exclusively in autographs and holographic material. It may or may not fascinate you personally but you should possess some knowledge of the subject. Similar material will come your way at times, usually as part of a large lot. You'll find holographic letters, post cards and such within books, obviously used as book marks. Learn what makes some worthless and others priceless. If nothing else, make arrangements to pass such items along to the specialist there at the fair.

Spend a bit of time with the dealer who handles nothing but old tracts and broadsheets. To me it's a mystifying branch of the business but you may be sure such things will sometimes come your way and it would be nice to have some vague idea of merit and values. You will probably have a hard time believing some of the prices you'll see on those ratty-looking old pamphlets but there's a brisk market there to be served. (If you think some books are scarce, stop and imagine how many copies of a two or three hundred year old leaflet are still around. This should help you understand those hefty price tags.)

Still to go is the post card booth, the dealer who specializes in hundred-year-old children's pop-up books and the stand featuring antiquarian maps. It's indeed a jolly holiday for the book fraternity.

About now you'll be asking yourself whether or not you should display at a fair yourself. The answer is probably yes, but not until you're ready. The price of a booth at a top fair may be as much as a thousand dollars. You'd have to be able to muster a fairly impressive offering to justify the expense. And before you commit to displaying at fairs you must become at ease with your own capabilities as a professional. You must be ready and able to field rapid-fire queries concerning you stock without having to duck under the counter for your references.

Depending upon your specialty, you should be able to begin with a small fair and feel your way comfortably up to the big time. I've paid as little as thirty-five dollars for a booth at regional science fiction fairs. The trick with fairs is to select only appropriate ones. That's simple enough if the fair has a set theme but most don't. Write to the organizer and find out something of the history of the fair. How long has it been held? What has been the level of sales realized in the past? Who else is already slated to display? If the fair has been around a while and has a history of good sales, if other dealers are going whom you believe share your type of stock, then it's probably worth going.

While it's perfectly true that the majority of dealers never display at a fair, I consider it another potent weapon in your arsenal of sales. There aren't that many ways I know of to realize an income well up into four, and possibly even five, figures over a weekend. If you know what you're doing, there's a great deal of money to be made at book fairs. Why do you think those dealers come all the way from Europe to take part? Unless you happen to be a rock star on the side, the rewards are such that you really ought to do some fairs when both you and your stock are up to it.

Another reason I believe fairs are vital is that it gets lonely out there sometimes. Sure, you have your customers, but we all share the need to talk ''shop'' sometimes. The sense of good fellowship alone is worth the trouble of attending. For those of us who invest in a booth, it's also a chance to sell those scarce collectable books that bombed out in our AB ads and quotes. It's absolutely true you can make sales in person which would be impossible through the mail. A scarce book which is flawed somehow often sounds terrible by the time you describe it completely and conservatively in an ad or a written quote. But in reality it might not look so unacceptable. At a fair a client might hold the book in his hand, note the imperfection, consider the price, and decide it's really a pretty nice copy for the money. He leaves and the transaction is complete. If the sale were conducted throught the mail there's a chance the book might come winging right back to you with a demand for a refund. Don't for a minute get the idea I'm suggesting you can sell rough books at a fair but it is a fact that we all tend to be far more conservative when ordering material through the mail.

A successful fair means careful planning. There's nothing more frustrating than being trapped alone behind your booth as the fair opens and discovering you forgot to bring your receipt book or whatever. Organizers should supply a list of necessary supplies. Books sold at a fair must always be wrapped at the time of sale so you'll require paper, tape, scissors. Find out exactly what display facilities are to be supplied by the fair committee and what you are expected to provide for yourself. Usually all they offer is one or two tables, so it's up to you to bring suitable shelving. The handiest and most attractive solution to the problem I know of is to invest in one of the authentic old lawyer's book cases. They are stackable and each shelf detaches, making an ideal display unit at a fair. If you are young and hardy you may even carry each unit complete with the books inside, ready for business.

If you never attend any other fairs as a buyer, don't miss the ABAA fairs, most often held in New York, Chicago, Los Angeles or San Franciso. You'll experience all the thrill of a kid in a candy store. I've watched fifty thousand dollars change hands for a small collection of T.E. Lawrence books, letters and memorabilia. I watched a man fork over ten thousand dollars for an unpublished holographic poem by T.S. Elliot. It gets your juices flowing and it's good for the soul. So go, meet your peers; warm your heart at the glow of good fellowship, tradition, and proud heritage of which you are now a part.

16

What Happens
When
I Want Out?

Some men speak of the loneliness of a life spent among books. If the great minds of the world are not companionable to him, a man in a library is indeed lonely. But the noise of many people trying hard to persuade themselves of their liveliness does not reassure me of my vitality. I find better assurance in the quiet voices of men who had something to say and could say it memorably. A man who can live within the sound of such voices lives doubly well. Indeed, in the narrow compass of the present he can hardly be said to live at all unless something from the past contribute to his understanding and judgment.

Sir Swante Palm

WHAT IS YOUR BOOK STORE WORTH?

The rule of thumb varies somewhat from one section of the country to another but they all seem to add up to about the same numbers so apparently the formula used matters little.

Possibly the most common method is to add the sum total of stock and fixtures, then add one year's net profit, and there you have a ball park estimate of value. Some brokers go by annual gross, which stikes me as stupid, given the enormous spread in profitability among businesses. Oddly enough, however, it still comes to about the same thing, at least in the case of used book stores.

Having employed whatever formula, you then get into the matter of variables which will either push the price upward or cause it to plummet. The terms and length remaining on your lease is vitally important. (If you haven't got a lease, either get one or plan on holding a going-out-of-business sale). Length of time you've been in business, or that the business has been there, will be another important consideration. The lengthier your track record and the healthier it looks, the more your business is worth. Part of what a buyer is paying for is Good Will; it is to be assumed there's more of that after ten years than there is after only one. (Not always a valid assumption, I'll admit). The changing pattern of the neighborhood will enter strongly into the computations as well. If you are located in a growth area, or at the very least a stable one, that will add some more icing on the cake. If your area is deemed to be suffering a decline, if the pattern of growth and future prosperity is away from you, this will lower the price considerably and almost certainly lengthen the time required to accomplish a sale.

Any visible defrayed maintenance will be tossed into the equation as well. Such things should be taken care of before even letting the listing broker see it so that you avoid getting gigged for it during his appraisal. You may as well, because any selling broker worth his salt will surely protect his buyers by putting it in the contract that everything on the premises must be functioning properly, any eyesores removed prior to close of escrow. The listing broker is responsible for the drawing up of a complete and accurate listing and the distribution of it, adequate advertising, and his full cooperation with other interested salespersons. It is also his job to look out for your interests as best he can, but in the end it is the buyer and his broker who end up in the driver's seat. Buyers have a tendency to be a little paranoid, and quite properly so. It's human nature for them to retain a clear image of the blemishes far more clearly than the beauty after seeing your shop. So touch up those paw prints around the door and the light switches. Stop that drip in the faucet even though the landlord does pay the water and you couldn't care less.

Avoid dealing with a broker who, when asked to suggest a fair and reasonable asking price, tells you he'll list it for whatever you want him to. He's just failed the first test and you can bet he'll fail others when you need him. An ethical, intelligent broker will perform his first and most vital service to you when he insures that you list the store at a price which is fair to both you and the buyer. He does you an enormous disservice if he allows you to put it up at a price which is unrealistic. This practice will almost inevitably result in your losing money on the sale. It encourages considerable negotiation, the submission of low offers, and keeps your shop on the market too long, allowing the listing to become stale in the eyes of the buyers and brokers as well. There is a magical "honeymoon" period lasting only a couple of months when a new listing is written. The fact that your business is NEW on the market piques the buyers' interest. It makes it easy for the selling broker to present it as something special, not likely to be equalled in value for a long time. But once that intital grace period passes, if your shop hasn't sold, it becomes just another one of the hundreds of dusty, half-forgotten listings cluttering up the salespeoples' books.

HOW TO CONVERT YOUR SHOP TO CASH

It's been my experience that it is actually quite simple. When you want out you should be able to get out with a hefty bundle of cash for your trouble.

Business brokers are no different from any others: stock brokers, housing brokers, yacht brokers, insurance brokers; they all have a ton of listings but most of them, in the immortal words of Alben Barkley when asked to describe the office of Vice President, aren't worth a bucket of warm spit. (I threw that in to offset all those grandiose quotes at the beginnings of chapters). Give a broker something of real value and you'll be lucky if he doesn't buy it himself. In my case that's exactly what happened once.

It may be helpful to walk you through my experiences in selling. I've sold three shops over the years. Two were in Southern California and one was located in the Midwest. Here is the way it worked for me each time I was ready to make a change. My first store was in San Diego. I called the largest business brokerage firm in town, offering to list it with them. An agent came by that very day and filled out the listing forms. In about a week the completed listing returned from their printer and was distributed among the salespersons within the brokerage firm. One of the brokers, a young woman, took one look at the listing, rushed over to my shop and handed me an Offer To Purchase form to sign. The buyer's name on the contract was hers. The price offered was my full asking price. I signed. As soon as she had satisfied herself that the listing was accurate she resigned from her office and became a bookseller. That was it! The ink never got a chance to dry on the finished listing, it never made it into the salespersons' listing books, was never advertised, and was never offered to a client.

My second store was also in San Diego. My wife and I had purchased a home in the Ozarks region of Missouri and had been spending more and more time back there and finally decided to move back full-time. Supposedly we were going to retire. Out of loyalty, we called the same listing agent we'd used the first time, though God knows he didn't really do anything. We had a little trouble running him down because he'd quit the big agency and gone independent. We listed with him again. Working out of his home, totally without office or staff, he found a buyer within three weeks. Once again the store sold for the full asking price. (Please don't start getting delusions of grandeur. The reason they sold for the full asking price is because we had priced them fairly in the first place.)

A few years later I began to get that restless urge again. There were already six used books stores in the city where I live. In a modest-sized town of just over a hundred thousand that might seem ample but not given the fact that there wasn't a single one being operated properly. Two were average, one was poor, and the other three terrible. (I'll let them figure out which they are.) From time to time I'd attempt to make constructive little suggestions. Nothing momentous, mind you; just things like, ''Why don't you save up and invest in a duster?'' No one cared or listened, so in November, 1983, just out of hospital and not feeling all that perky, I said ENOUGH and decided to give the town a proper antiquarian book shop. I also figured it would be good therapy for what ailed me and I was right.

Utilizing the same guidelines given earlier in this book, I found a location and set to work. It was scarcely an ideal spot but I only had a couple of weeks before the deadline for the ads in the local telephone company Yellow Pages. I wasn't willing to begin a new company and wait a year for an ad in the phone book. My space was in a sleepy little shopping center consisting of about nine small stores, none of which drew many people. The saving factor was that it was on the third most-heavily traveled street in the city. I completed all the construction alone; opening day was January 5th, 1984. There was a blizzard that day and I sold six dollars worth of books. The second day I got lucky and did twenty-four dollars.

By April I was netting four thousand dollars a month and my gross sales were in excess of those other six stores combined. Let this give you food for thought if you find yourself considering opening a shop in your hometown.

Never mind how many other shops already exist. How many GOOD ones are there?

By the middle of May it became apparent that I was going to have to return to the hospital for lots of fun tests and probable surgery. I called the largest business brokerage office in town and they dispatched a broker to come out and talk to me. After asking me a few general questions she shook her head and informed me that it would be impossible to sell a five-month-old fledgling business with such a limited track record. I handed her the books, together with a graph I'd drawn showing showing weekly sales increases expressed in a curve. I watched her beady eyes widen; no wonder — it looked like the highway to heaven. I told her I thought we'd better sell it now because the way things were going, in another year there wouldn't be too many buyers who could afford it.

Escrow closed on my third and last store on June 14th, 1984, five and a half months from the opening date. As before, I received my full asking price; the buyer, a bright and enthusiastic ex-school teacher, just managed to beat out one of the firm's brokers who was working up his nerve to buy it.

So, as you can see, converting your shop into cash when the time arrives doesn't seem to be a problem. I have seen shops listed which have failed to sell but never if the shop were SALEABLE. The truth of the matter is, in those areas with which I'm familiar, fine antiquarian book shops tend to remain under the same ownership for a very long time and it's quite an occasion when one does come on the market.

This brings us to the question of whether or not you should consider buying an established shop rather than starting one from scratch. I've done it both ways and I'd never buy a going concern again. The cost is too great when you consider how little it runs to start your own from square one. It would make sense if, as in most businesses, there was a long start up time involved but you can see that's not the case. And if you buy someone else's shop you'll probably never be quite satisfied with the layout or the quality of the shelves or many other things you'd have done differently. I know my first store nearly drove me nuts because it was built out of junk lumber and the shelves were all the wrong sizes and there were no backs to the shelving so when you pushed a book onto the shelf too hard it fell over into the next aisle.

The other side of the coin, though, is I'd never have known what I needed or how to go about doing it right if I hadn't bought that first store.

My whole motive for writing this book is to prevent other neophyte booksellers from having to buy second or third rate shops rather than create their own in such a way that they'll surely prosper.

Now let me say, if funding is not a problem and you just don't want to bother with building all those shelves, there are certainly some superb shops around and if you're very, very lucky, one might even come on the market when you're ready. If so, grab it! If it's a good operation, you're not going to have too long to think about it.

YOUR OBLIGATIONS TO THE BUYER WHEN YOU SELL

Chances are when you sell, the contract will contain a Non-Compete clause. Normally this guarantees the buyer you will not go into the same business within five miles for five years from the date of the closing of the sale. This is common practice for obvious reasons. Stories are legion about those who sell a business for a hefty price, then open up across the street and drive the buyer under. It's a protection the buyer has every right to expect and I believe it's your obligation to give it. There will also be some means of indemnifying the buyer against bills or demands originating prior to the sale which could become a lien against the business. This is standard because most small businesses depend upon wholesalers or manufacturers for their stock and billing is sometimes delayed as much as ninety days. It's a little inappropriate in the case of a used book store but you may expect it and it's nothing to worry about.

I've already mentioned the contingency about all systems being functional at closing of escrow. All this means is all the lights and the plumbing should work.

The one hassle you may run into with an inexperienced broker is a demand for an inventory. I helped a friend who was selling his store do an inventory once and I never want to do so again. The trouble is it's usually common practice, so the selling broker may feel it's proper to demand it in order to protect his clients. It's an exhausting exercise in futility; accomplishing nothing. For one thing the stock changes so rapidly it'll be outdated before it's finished. For another, unlike most retail businesses, you've got so little actual cash tied up in stock, it isn't worthwhile to perform an inventory. The only possible reason a buyer has for wanting an inventory would be fear that you might remove some of the stock prior to close of escrow. It has always been my experience that the rapport between the principals in these transactions is such that no such fear will exist. It is the policy of some brokers to keep the principals separated as much as possible until the transaction is complete but don't let them do it. You are going to have a very special and ongoing relationship with the buyer and the sooner it establishes itself the better.

This brings us to your real obligation to the buyer, which only begins after the sale. As a part of that purchase price which you now have tucked away in the bank, you owe that poor lost soul who bought your store a complete course of instruction in every phase of bookselling. I've always guaranteed my buyers a full thirty days of full-time instruction. It shouldn't actually take that long but it gives them a sense of security. It's an intense period for both parties and problems can occur. You mustn't be so rigid that any slight variations from your methods cause you to correct the buyer. You must realize it's important as the days go by for the new operator to impress his own personality on the shop and he'll accomplish this by doing some things differently. Some will be improvements; some won't. The bookseller who sold me my first store gave me a wonderfully thorough period of training but towards the end, when I began making some changes, she became so incensed that I would alter a single thing she walked out of the store and swore she'd never set foot in it again. That was many years ago and insofar as I know, she never has.

So don't be so silly and vain as to become offended as your buyer begins to spread his own wings and make the store his own. That's exactly what you want to happen. As a practical matter, two weeks is more than adequate for this transitional training period but make yourself available for the full month if the buyer desires it. Even beyond this, plan to stop by the shop occasionally and encourage the new owner to feel free to call and ask questions as unusual situations come up. The final thing they'll need from you is to confer on exceptional material which they aren't comfortable pricing. And make certain you go out with them at least once to bid on a library because this can be an overwhelming thing to a neophyte.

Beyond that, the only other thing you may or may not want to do is to offer your services in case of illness or to work a day or two a week until they can find and train an assistant. This is a great source of security for a new owner to have and I encourage you to do it if your schedule allows. It's also a pleasant experience for you because, no matter how much you may think you want to be free of the shop when you finally sell, you're going to miss it more than you can ever imagine.

17

Most
Common
Mistakes

Books — you are wonderful. In you live the hope, the comfort, the philosophy, the glory, the peace, the reward of a world. You line the edge of my life. As I view you — of a thousand lives expressed and of a hundred thousand thoughts revealed — I say that come what may, so long as I stick to you, I shall not be entirely alone.

George Matthew Adams

For those of you who are determined to screw up a foolproof guide to success, I dedicate this chapter. If you are expiating some nameless childhood guilt or perhaps just terrified of hitting the upper tax brackets, the suggestions contained herein will serve you well. The experts tell us there are those who fear success and will go to any lengths to avoid it but you're going to have to work hard to fail as a bookseller so pay attention.

I certainly don't mean to say there isn't a successful antiquarian book shop in the entire country that violates a single one of these precepts but, believe me, if they do it's hurting them. There is absolutely no reason on earth any well-run shop can't eliminate every solitary one of the shortcomings listed below. Each one is a little kiss of death. The really sad part is that the vast majority of existing stores are guilty of some, and in most cases many, of them. On the other hand, maybe it's not so sad; that's why such a golden opportunity exists for you.

Overpricing: There are a great many stores which charge 60 per cent of the cover price for general stock paperbacks, particularly nonfiction. Others tack on a 5 or 10 cent cash surcharge for every book taken out on trade. Such stores routinely charge 60 per cent of the in-print price for contemporary, easy-to-find hardbacks. Many really go for the jugular on ANY out-of-print book, no matter how common or uninteresting. Terrific way to save yourself a lot of work. Do this and there'll be so few books coming in and going out you'll have plenty of time to catch up on your own reading.

Inappropriate Stock: The simplest thing in the world to do is set up a used book shop and fill the shelves with book club novels, Reader's Digest Condensed Books, textbooks and shabby, dirty or coverless paperbacks. In fact it's so easy that people all across the country have done just that. You'll know them when you meet them; they're the ones who are forever lamenting that there isn't any money to be made in the used book business. A book is seldom neutral; either it's an asset or it's a liability. Read this book carefully and follow through with one or more of the recommended publications. Learn to tell the difference and, last of all, trust your instincts.

Books Not Arranged in Logical Sequence: Most stores at least establish subject sections though, hard to believe I know, I have seen more than a few that simply sling them on the shelf (or floor) and the rest is up to you. Where so many stores fail is they don't take the trouble to alphabetize their books by author within the subject sections. Admittedly it's a bit of a chore in the beginning but once done it's very easy to maintain and there's nothing you could do which would garner you half as much gratitude from your customers or do nearly so much to increase your income. Some stores like to lay their books down flat and pile them one on top of the other. They embrace the theory that many of the titles are more easily read this way. The truth is it tears hell out of the books every time they're handled and it's impossible to keep them in alphabetical order. This method is the certain sign of a lazy amateur; you will never see it done this way in any really prosperous shop.

Stale Stock: Not even Babe Ruth batted a thousand and neither will you. In contrast to most retail businesses, your inventory cost is such that your mistakes can't really hurt you as long as you have the guts and good sense to get rid of them. It may not cost you much to acquire stock but it runs you plenty to warehouse it for long periods of time. The true cost is the lack of turnover and income, along with the featuring of poor quality material. Monitor your titles; when you get tired of looking at a book either mark it down if it has enough merit or out to the bargain rack with it. Be very careful to never let your regular customers become bored with your offering. Too much depends upon too few for you to ever let that happen. New material will constantly continue arriving but the only way you may accept it is to move out the old. If you ever find yourself having to turn down good incoming trades or sales you're somehow blowing it.

Never show duplicates on your shelves. It's human nature that a buyer will feel there's no hurry about buying, there will always be a copy available when he wants it. Buy all the duplicates of good solid material you can but stash the extras in the back room, not side-by-side on the shelf.

Books in Unsaleable Condition: This is not only one of the most common failings of antiquarian shops, it is also one of the most unforgivable. Shabby, worn paperbacks on the shelf are nothing less than stupid; you'd have to keep turning down mint-condition books in order to maintain the space for them. I understand HOW it happens; I just don't understand WHY it happens. If you accept beat-up books along with sharp material, the nice copies sell and you're left with the junk. Please be selective, especially in the case of very common stock such as paperback fiction. You may rest assured your customers are going to be most selective. Stocking rough books is one of the best ways I know of driving them away forever.

The same is true of hardback books. It is true you don't apply quite the same standards to a two hundred year old book as you would to a ten year old book, but even the former must be tight in the binding, spine legible and intact, clean and free of moisture stains or mildew. Some foxing, the brown acid stains which come with aging, is acceptable. Your contemporary books should have dust wrappers unless they are of more than average interest, (assuming they were issued with wrappers; most but not all are.). By the time you begin talking about pre-nineteen thirty, wrappers will begin to become scarce, so you can't expect to follow this dictum but you'll always find a book with a wrapper will sell many times more quickly and bring more than the same book without one.

If you've ever attempted to read a book that's been underlined with pen or pencil or highlighted with a yellow marker, you realize how annoying and distracting it is. No such defaced book should ever be found on your shelf. It's not **uncommon** to find books offered in the children's section which have been scribbled in or used as coloring books. Such stores — together with their proprietors — are a blight upon this entire industry.

A bookplate or signature of the previous owner is not considered a flaw and may be overlooked.

Unclean Store: Not to belabor the obvious but there are an incredible number of filthy shops around. Make certain the books are clean before they go on the shelf. You can really minimize the problem if you just remember to change your air conditioner and heater filters monthly. There's absolutely nothing charming or intriguing about a shop where your hands and clothing become dirty from handling the books. Some people will tolerate this from a thrift store where all books are uniformly priced at a quarter or fifty cents but certainly not in the sort of shop this book is concerned with. It's true books aren't the easiest thing in the world to keep clean if yours is a dusty environment but a feather duster diligently used is all that's required. Of course your best defense is to keep that stock turning over quickly.

Mad At The World: You can incorporate all the information within this book and still end up with a mediocre business by the simple expedient of snarling at your customers. Be smart enough to be honest with yourself before committing to this or any other enterprise which places you eyeball-to-eyeball with the public. If you are a natural born curmudgeon, stay out of retail sales. I knew a man once who used to sit behind his counter and watch daytime television while his store was open. Every time a customer came in he'd either ignore them or give them a dirty glance as if they were interrupting something important. As you may have guessed, his career as a bookseller was a brief one.

There are some others I've seen who tend to become pedantic or ridicule those who ask them admittedly silly questions. This gets into that tendency to elitism I mentioned earlier. Such swipes at your customers are inappropriate and counter-productive. If you can't get your act together and appreciate your clientele it's going to hurt you in direct ratio to the seriousness of your own personal hangups.

Poor Location: Very common error; to save a couple of hundred dollars in rent by locating in low-traffic or declining area. Very bright. Undoubtedly costs you many tens of thousands of dollars annually in lost sales revenue. Also makes your shop worth little if anything when you go to sell. Does offer some advantages: you won't have to look up from your book too often to wait on a customer and you won't have to worry about making change for any large bills.

Run A Tight Ship: Some shops give the impression of having walked into the Pentagon. Their walls are plastered with the most nasty, negative messages imaginable. No doubt they wonder why there is such a funereal air about the place. Some of my favorites are: "Ten dollar charge for all returned checks." "All packages must be left at the front counter." "No refunds; all sales are final." "You are responsible for all damage you cause." "No personal checks."

You might just as well put up one big sign proclaiming the obvious fact that you don't give a damn for your customers, certainly don't trust them, and aren't about to go an inch out of your way for them. There isn't an example given above that doesn't take a big bite out of the gross of any shop. If you feel compelled to put up any signs at all, find a way to express your message in a friendly, positive way. Such signs are one of the very first ways in which people will judge you and your store. One of the great verities of life is that other people are not much different than you. They all want to be treated with respect, warmth and trust. If you open an antiquarian book shop you will be fortunate enough to be able to accord them this treatment, so don't screw it all up with a lot of unnecessary insulting messages.

Illogical Hours: One of the simplest means of controlling your income is by adjusting your hours. Many shops are marginal due to inappropriate hours. Some even open and close pretty much when they feel like it. You may imagine how successful they are. I know a man who opens at two in the afternoon and closes at five. He used to be open longer but he kept lopping off hours as his business dropped off. At this point, there's little reason to be open at all and he won't be for very long. A friend of mine had virtually the same problem — both dealers are located in the same city and the slowdown came with the recession of the late '70s — but he handled his differently. He began staying open later at night. Instead of closing at 6:00 P.M. he remained open until 8:00. It became quite a popular evening outing for people in his area to stroll over to his shop after dinner and browse. His sales soared. Two different solutions to the same problem. Two different personalities. One negative and defeatist and the other aggressive and confident. That's all there is to say. So it's always been and so it will always be.

The point is, select your hours to suit your clientele, not yourself. If you're in a shopping center the hours will be pretty much set already. There isn't much point in remaining open after the center has gone dark and everyone else has gone home. But don't allow yourself to be so self-indulgent you open at 11:00 A.M. when every other store is open at 10:00 A.M. Keep your hours simple and logical so that your customers have some chance of remembering them. The best method by far is to open the same hours every day, including Sunday. Most shops are closed on Sundays in spite of the fact it is one of the few days families have the time to shop together in a way that is most lucrative for this business. I've always been open on Sunday, enjoyed a monopoly on the market that day, and prospered. Remember the only increase in your overhead is the salary you'll pay someone to work Sundays. And you simplify things for your customers if all they have to remember is that you're open EVERY DAY!

The Everything Store Is Nothing: If you really want to confuse, discourage and drive away your customers, never miss an opportunity to stock every hare-brained product anyone promotes to you. Move some of those books out and put in games or greeting cards. How about some stationery? Piles of old magazines lying around on the floor are good, too. I've seen all these things and a lot more. But never in a shop that was worthy of the name. Here's another sure-fire method to drive your store right into the ground.

Inappropriate Specialization: This is not such a common failing but I have seen it happen, so it bears mentioning. Sometimes we become so wrapped up in our own interests we can't appreciate the fact that it's of little or no interest to those around us. We all know examples of the person who has a one-track-mind, a Johnny One-Note who doesn't seem to be able to talk about anything other than his one all-consuming passion. That's bad enough, but in the book business it would very likely be fatal. Let me give you an example: a dealer I used to know was totally fascinated with the subject of metaphysics. It was all he read, cared for or talked about. He opened a shop, specializing in metaphysical material. Sure, he developed a loyal little coterie of clients who thought the world of him and his shop but the specialty he'd chosen was so limited in its appeal there was no conceivable way he could ever succeed except in the most modest way. You'd think he'd have known that, wouldn't you? But it sometimes happens that our pet enthusiasms override our logic and good sense. That's what it means to be passionate about something, after all. Specialize, sure; salve your own pet interests. But don't neglect to do as much for those whom you expect to support you in the style to which you would like to become accustomed — your customers.

18
Just
for
Fun!

What a joy there is in a good book, writ by some great master of thought, who breaks in beauty as in summer the meadows into grass and dandelions and violets with geraniums and manifold sweetness.

Theodore Parker

They say close only counts in horeshoes and hand grenades; I guess it's true. Let me tell you about the time I just missed out on about fifteen million dollars.

The first shop I ever owned was being managed by my assistant, a comely lass of tender years. One of our stranger customers was a short chubby fellow of late middle age. His courtly manners endeared him to all of us, but failed to disguise the fact that he was missing a couple of bolts. Or as my assistant put it, "He's got a drift factor of about seven." He looked a lot like one of the Ritz Brothers — the one with the "wide part" — and it was apparent he was becoming increasingly enamoured with my employee. We had named him "Rare Books" because he often referred to his vast library of rare books. This in spite of the fact that he was dressed in shabby clothes and the only books he ever took out of the store were from the FREE BOX. My employee figured the only reason he came around and sweet-talked her was to get free books.

Finally the day came, as I came in to relieve her, when she held her sides to keep them from splitting and informed me he'd asked her to run away with him. In light of the fact that he was more than twice her age — nearer triple — and rowing up the stream of life with only one oar, I had to admit there was a certain humor there. Understand, this was one capable young lady who wasn't about to be intimidated by any man. (I'd once seen her explain something twice to a guy who didn't know how to listen, so she jammed her face six inches in front of his and told him in a loud, evenly-spaced voice: "Hey, you; READ MY LIPS!''

In spite of the fact she was married, she typically elected to use me as the scapegoat. (Half the fun of working together is setting one another up.) She told the poor soul she didn't dare because I would hunt them down to the ends of the earth if she were to leave. Just when I thought I was all laughed out she told me the best part. He'd confided to her in a stage whisper the solemn fact that he possessed no fewer than ten Gutenberg Bibles.

I thought it a royal chuckle but the best was yet to come. The following day the fellow returned while I was at the counter and asked if he might discuss a serious matter with me. Between bouts of silence whenever a client came up to pay for his books, he made his pitch. If I would give my blessing to his wooing of my assistant, he would be willing to bestow upon me some of the priceless Gutenbergs. Without batting an eye, I entered into furious negotiations. I held out for no fewer than six books, with the firm understanding that I was to select the six I wanted from the lot of ten. His heart betrayed him and in the end he capitulated. With a reluctant sigh, I gave him my blessing. As he left, I noticed he was wearing one blue and one brown sock under his battered tennies. A match surely made in heaven, I thought.

When my manager came in the next day I informed her of the agreement and said I would understand if she were to close early one night soon. I guess I should have offered to share the wealth because she apparently found a way to get through to the guy that she was not going to fulfill his fantasies. Alas, I never saw him again. And that's how — due to the perfidy of a woman — I came to lose millions.

Another woman cost me a somewhat lesser amount. My wife loved working in the shop, though she was more interested in the conviviality than in the collectable material. One day a young man walked up to my counter with a dazed look on his face and handed me two dollars. The item he was purchasing was a thin little cartoon-format wrapped volume by Vaughn Bode entitled, *Mein Kamph*. On the back of the booklet it stated that this was one of three hundred, printed by hand press in the apartment of the author in Greenwich Village. I knew Bode, who had died tragically in his early twenties, was an important cult hero among certain collectors and I knew the insignificant-looking little book was currently valued at around three hundred dollars. I'll admit I was in agony but there's only one thing to do under such circumstances. The cover price was $2.95 so I sold him the book for $1.50. Only after he was sure the transaction was completed, the fellow confessed he'd never expected to find a copy or, finding one, be able to afford it. He asked whether I knew what it was worth. I told him I did, but that I liked to hide such gems among the general stock just to drive the collectors nuts.

My wife remembered taking *Mein Kamph* in on trade one day while she was on the desk. Typically, she had no regrets that we'd had to sell it for one half of one per cent of its value; she only felt badly for the person who'd brought it in.

This next little anecdote gave me more satisfaction than just about any transaction I can remember. I was driving down a residential street in San Diego one day when I noticed a sign saying BOOKS. A man was carrying out cardboard boxes of books from his garage and arraying them on his lawn. Of course I stopped. The fellow informed me he was a collector and he was offering many valuable first editions. I began scanning the boxes as he carried them out; there were a handful of first editions but none with wrappers. The authors represented were not of interest anyway and the vast majority of the books were obviously book clubs. His prices were ridiculous, so I pointed this out to him in order to save him embarrassment and a waste of time. He haughtily informed me he was an expert on collectable books, thank you very much, and turned and stomped off.

As I left I noticed a lovely little girl of perhaps six sitting under a tree in the far corner of the yard. A circle of what appeared to be books ringed her. Naturally I couldn't resist going over for a look. I asked her if she was having a book sale just like her daddy. She shyly informed me this was so. I asked her the price of her books and she told me more sternly they were twenty-five cents each, as if to let me know the price was not negotiable. My mind wasn't on haggling; it was focused upon three of the books lying there on the grass. Among her children's books were three *Wizard of Oz* titles in what appeared to be first edition format. I didn't take them to be firsts because the older reprints are far more common, but even those with all the wonderful color plates and pictorial cover are worth fifty or sixty dollars. The books were all in VG condition. I was reluctant to take advantage of the child but it's up to a seller to price his wares. A couple of women dragging children were approaching, so I gathered up the OZ books and handed her three dollars, telling her I thought she'd priced the books a little low.

Back in the shop, I got out my OZ reference and checked the points on the books. Sure enough, one of the books was a first edition, first issue. I was wishing I'd been more generous to the girl before but now I felt an obligation. The first was worth around a hundred and fifty dollars. I feel the ethics of my profession demand that when someone offers me a collectable book in my shop it's up to me to tell them what they have and pay a fair price. It's true I didn't buy the OZ book in the store and I don't usually feel obliged to educate people outside my shop but this was unique. She was a six-year-old girl. (If only I'd bought the books from daddy; there would be no moral dilemma whatsoever.)

That evening after closing, I returned to the house and asked to speak to the child. With her parents hovering over us, I handed the little girl four twenty dollar bills, telling her, ''This is for one of the really nice books you sold me today. I checked and found it's a scarce first edition worth about a hundred and fifty dollars. Your daddy must not have seen it or he would have known that, since he's an expert.''

The look on the child's face was worth the price but I'll never forget the expression on her father's face. After a day of trying to sell his ''collectables'' I'm sure he now knew his precious library was all but worthless. And now he finds out one of his daughter's story books is worth real money. I watched his chin hit his chest and his eyes bug. His wife followed my gaze and burst out laughing. It was an altogether satisfying moment.

Yes, I know what you're thinking: it doesn't make me a saint because I went back and gave the child more money; I only did it to gig the father. And you're at least half right.

This final tale is not only amusing but instructive as well. There was a bookseller in a nearby town who had a reputation for ''sharp practices'', meaning he wasn't considered reliable. It was always my custom to visit other shops and check over their stock carefully for mistakes — firsts or important books they'd not recognized and that were underpriced.

One day I was in this man's store when I noticed a copy of Michener's wonderful book on Japanese prints, *Floating Worlds*. I knew I had a want in my files for the book, so I asked how much the book was. For some reason it was behind the counter where I couldn't get at it. He gave me a wary look and replied he hadn't had time to research it yet and asked me what I'd put on it. I told him a hundred and fifty dollars was about right (this was quite a few years ago), knowing I'd blown all chance of getting a bargain. He asked if I wanted it for that, less my usual 20 per cent discount. I said I'd have to pass, since there was every likelihood I'd end up selling it to a dealer as well and thus end up breaking even.

When I'd rounded up my stack of books to buy and was ready to leave, he offered the Michener to me for one hundred dollars. It was pristine, still in its heavy slipcase. I told him to add it to my pile.

Back in my store a day or two later, I called the client in my files and told her I'd come up with a copy of *Floating Worlds*. She asked me the price; I told her one hundred and fifty dollars. She laughed and said she'd already found one and that she'd only paid a third of that. I congratulated her on her good fortune.

About a week later this same woman and her husband entered the store. She looked angry. They told me they'd found a copy of *Floating Worlds* at another shop but didn't have their check book with them, so they put down one-third of the fifty dollar purchase price in cash and arranged to redeem the book within a week. When they went back the book was gone. The owner of the shop had told them the lay-away slip must have fallen out of the book and his wife had sold it, not realizing it was already sold. Of course he'd given them back their deposit.

Almost shaking with anger as she told me this, she then asked whether I still had my copy. I handed it to her. She stood there staring at it in disbelief. She handed it to her husband and told him it was the same book she'd bought before. When I asked how she could be certain she said she knew by the crumpled corner at the bottom of the slipcase. Then she took the book from her husband and handed it back to me. Neither of them had removed the book from its box. She said there was a book plate with the former owner's name inside the front cover. Giving me the name, she asked me to open the book and check. The name was there, just as she described it.

It was obvious what had happened: when the sly proprietor of the other shop realized he'd sold the book too cheaply he simply opted to double his money and lie to his customers. Except he'd been caught! The couple were steamed; she was all for taking the guy to Small Claims Court. (That was only after her husband and I told her we thought tarring and feathering was out.)

In order to try and restore their faith in booksellers I offered to let them have the book for just what I'd paid for it — one hundred dollars. For a brief moment I'd considered covering for the other dealer when she asked me whether I'd bought the book from the man or his wife. From the man, I told her. She'd nodded, knowing then as a certainty that there hadn't been any honest mistake.

The dealer in question soon wore out his welcome in those parts and went out of business after trying unsuccessfully to sell the shop. I heard he started up again in another city at the other end of the state. He probably didn't last very long there either unless he found out engaging in "sharp" deals for a few extra "fast" bucks isn't going to work in this business. Your clientele is too bright, intuitive and small in number compared with most retail stores. Lines of communication are to well-defined and cross too often. Your customers also shop in other book stores. They talk to people there who also know you. Experiences and impressions and opinions will be exchanged freely concerning you and your methods of doing business. You will rise or fall in this industry as a direct result of the consensus which will emerge. Play straight with your customers and they'll take you right to the top.

19

Ready
Reference
to Suppliers

AMERICAN BOOK PRICES CURRENT
121 E. 78th Street
New York, NY 10021

An excellent set of price guides giving reliable information.

ANTIQUARIAN BOOKMAN (AB)
Box AB
Clifton, NJ 07015

A weekly book trade news and feature magazine that also lists books
wanted by dealers all over the world. It offers an opportunity to quote
and sell fine material which you may not have an active market for in
your shop. It also lists books for sale, usually at dealers' prices giving you
a chance to enhance your own offering and fill the scarcer wants of your
clients. The AB is a must for any full-service antiquarian book store.

THE BOOKMAN'S GLOSSARY
R.R. Bowker Company
62 W. 45th Street
New York, NY

An inexpensive and essential guide to the blizzard of foreign terms to be
encountered in the trade.

BOOKMAN'S PRICE INDEX SERIES
Gale Research Inc.
835 Penobscot Building
Detroit, MI 48226-4094

An excellent series of price guides with reliable information.

BOOKQUEST/SERIALS
ABACIS, Inc.
135 Village Queen Drive
Owings Mills, MD 21117

This is an online database which provides listings for rare and out-of-print books.

BOOKQUOTE
2319-C West Rohmann
Peoria, IL 61604-5072

A book trade bi-weekly for buyers and sellers of used and rare books.

BOOK SOURCE MONTHLY
P.O. Box 567
Cazenovia, NY 13035-0567

A monthly trade publication with listings, calendars and reviews.

BOWKER'S BOOKS IN PRINT
R.R. Bowker
245 West 17th Street
New York, NY 10011

This is an annual reference which comes in a pair of two volume sets, one set giving all the current books in print referenced by author and the other referenced by title. It is helpful to an antiquarian bookseller in several ways: it tells you whether or not a given book is in or out of print; it tells you the retail price of a book which bears no publisher's price. This is helpful in establishing an appropriate price for the book in your shop. You can easily buy a year or two old edition from one of your local new book shops or find a set offered in an AB ad.

BRODART, CO.
1609 Memorial Avenue
Williamsport, PA 17705

This is an excellent library supply house offering just anything and everything the well-equipped shop would ever need. Most common items ordered from Brodart include mylar jackets to protect dust wrappers of collectable books, book ends, signs designating subject sections, stands used to display books in an open position, and step stools. A note on your letterhead requesting a catalogue will be responded to promptly.

THE BUYER'S GUIDE
700 E. State Street
Iola, WI 54990

This is a weekly sales periodical featuring mostly comics and comic art. But it is well worth the nineteen dollar annual subscription rate to pick up the hardback books also being offered by private collectors. It is also your source for the five by seven inch plastic bags used to protect your collectable paperbacks. Most of the titles to be found will be within the genre of science fiction and horror fantasy, so if this doesn't interest you there's little point in subscribing.

FIRST EDITIONS: A GUIDE TO IDENTIFICATION
The Spoon River Press
2319-C West Rohmann Avenue
Peoria, IL 61604

An absolute must in order to wade through the maze of publishers' often esoteric, apparently clandestine and forever changing methods of designating first editions.

INTERNATIONAL RARE BOOK PRICES
The Spoon River Press
2319-C West Rohmann
Peoria, IL 61604

A series giving US and British book prices and trade contacts.

MANDEVILLE'S USED BOOK PRICE GUIDE
P.O. Box 82525
Kenmore, WA 98028

Available as a two volume set published in 1972 or as an updated reference complete in one volume published in 1977 or the most recent issued in 1983. I believe this guide is based on catalogue prices, as opposed to auction prices, so it may not have quite the desirability of some. In other words, it is based upon "asking" prices rather than prices realized at the time of sale. On the other hand, auction prices may sometimes be quite low so this guide might be the better reference for your store values. The most recent issue is a five-year edition published in 1989.

OFFICIAL PRICE GUIDE TO PAPERBACKS AND MAGAZINES
House of Collectibles, Inc.
Orlando Central Park
1900 Premier Row
Orlando, FL 32809

SOTHEBY'S
1334 York Avenue at 72nd Street
New York, NY 10021

You may subscribe to Sotheby's auction catalogues annually and receive
the realized prices after the sale at no extra cost. Their sales include
books, manuscripts and autographs. The service, while fascinating reading for anyone in the industry, isn't going to be much help as a general
price guide. Still, it's helpful to keep abreast of the top auction results
and you may decide to ship material of your own to Sotheby's for auction.
If you decide to do so, write them first with full descriptions to obtain
permission to ship.

INDEX